Citizens for Trump

JACK POSOBIEC

ISBN:154693653X
ISBN-13:9781546936534

DEDICATION

This book is dedicated to the deplorables.

CONTENTS

ACKNOWLEDGMENTS

To everyone who's ever given me a chance, to everyone who's ever retweeted or shared a post, to everyone who's ever opened a livestream, to my friends and family and my darazhenkaja who waited for me for so many long nights on the campaign trail.

Many thanks as well to Erica Setnick, Trevor Wright, and Lorrie Posobiec for helping me turn a mountain of unintelligible ramblings into a book for humans.

Also, a special thanks to the mainstream media, the Left, and the global elites for telling us every day we couldn't do it, just so we could prove you all wrong and have the most amazing year of our lives doing it.

1. INTRODUCTION

This is not a book about Donald Trump. Many books have been written about Donald Trump. Even more have been written about how he won the 2016 presidential election. This is a book about the people. The people who threw their support behind Trump. The people who got fed up and decided to do something about it. The people who spent countless hours and their own dollars, footsteps, gas tanks, and data plans working tirelessly to help Trump win the election. The movement they created. They are the true heroes of 2016, and this is their book. This is a book about the movement that grew tired of the two main political parties in America, swelled up organically, and propelled Donald Trump as their champion into the highest office in the land. Whether you are a Trump supporter, a Trump hater, or just someone who wants to understand what happened in 2016, this book is your way to learn how the movement began – whether you like it or not.

One of the main differences between the Trump movement and other movements in politics is that the Trump movement is first and foremost a movement of the people. There hasn't been a force whatsoever in politics before the Trump insurgency that has been so widespread or so successful. The reason that the Trump movement was so widespread and so successful is simply because now, the levers of power have changed, and the monopoly on news of the mainstream media has dissipated with the arrival of social media.

Never before in America have so many people been able to connect in such a way as they have with Twitter, Facebook and Instagram – among others. Also, never before have people had a way to share news and information that was not being covered by the so called 'mainstream' media, the traditional television news programs that most of us grew up with. The difference has been revolutionary.

This election has shaped so many new paths, especially with the help of social media. Citizen journalists have shared unfiltered, unedited, raw news footage with the help of a live-streaming video application called Periscope, and are on track to become the new trusted way Americans get their information. Regardless of your politics, Donald Trump as a litmus test has proven how biased the mainstream media is, and with that, comes the rise of citizen journalism. The American people are taking their country back, and they're taking their news back.

FDR won through his mastery of radio, JFK won through mastering television, and Donald Trump became the president of the United States through his mastery of social media.

It is ironic that, at the same time in which American people were beginning to connect and share information in new and revolutionary innovative ways, that the mainstream media would instead be seeking to change the narrative to put out false information to lie, to confuse and to generally create psychological operations (psy-ops) against the American people and against Donald Trump. These psy-ops will be covered in detail and were used viciously by the mainstream media against Donald Trump and his supporters.

The differences between this book and other books are that those books will talk to you about Donald Trump and Hillary Clinton as specific people, meanwhile, in this book, I am going to be talking about this race from the perspective of somebody who lived it, from somebody who was on the inside in many ways, from someone who traveled the country working within the Donald Trump People's movement to bring it to the final victory. I'll be able to share inside stories from along the way, share anecdotes from some people that you've all heard of, some that you haven't heard of, but you'll be able to know the important role they played in bringing Donald Trump's success to the White House.

But before all that, let's do some background.

So just who the heck is Jack Posobiec, anyway? If you're anything like me, you like to know who it is that is writing the book that you're currently reading. Whenever I read a book, I always go to the back flap and read that little bit of blurb that says "about the author" or I'll go online to look on Wikipedia and find out a little more about the author, their mindset, and their frame of reference while they write. I like to know who put the words on this page that I'm reading right now. Sometimes you find out very interesting things about the author, and sometimes you find out things that make you very upset. Hopefully there's nothing that I have in my background that makes you upset, but if there isn't - I'll just have to try harder.

My full name is John Michael Posobiec III. I go by Jack. I was born in Norristown, Pennsylvania in 1984. It's a small, urban town about fifteen miles outside of Philadelphia. Norristown is located in Montgomery County and it is one of the five collar counties of Philadelphia. If you've heard of Valley Forge or King of Prussia, it's very very close to there. Both my mom and my dad are from the same area, and my brother Kevin lives there too.

(Posobiec Family visit to NYC, 1991)

I went to Temple University and graduated with a double-major in broadcasting mass media and political science. I also attended the Aresty Institute of Leadership at the Wharton School of Business, University of Pennsylvania.

Working in politics is not something that I ever sought out to do. I never thought I had an interest in politics when I was younger—even in high school—nor had I thought I had an interest in government whatsoever. I always wanted to be a filmmaker, or a writer, or an actor. I really enjoy being creative, I really enjoy performing—especially live—and I really enjoy being able to entertain people and share that love of performance with them. I did my first stand-up comedy act at age 8, in front of my entire grade school. I tried my hand at it some more when I got older, at clubs in Philadelphia. A lot of fun!

But then I got to college. When I first got there, I looked around and I saw some of the people, I started to listen to them. Not just the students but the professors, the people we were supposed to look up to, to be our role models in these institutions of higher learning. And the main thing I couldn't help but think was, *are these people nuts?* I thought that they were saying some of the most off-the-wall zaniest things that I could think of, and no one was disagreeing. It was like an echo chamber.

When we were in class, for example, one of the general elective classes you have to take was called Introduction to American Politics. I realized early on that something was wrong. Very, very wrong.

Something just didn't sit right. What I was learning didn't seem to make sense. So, I started to get more informed about politics. I started to read more, listen to the radio more, research more, and dig deeper into the issues of who exactly these politician were that were running our country, and who exactly these parties were and what they stood for. I noticed very early on that I was closer to the Republican Party than the Democratic Party.

The Republican Party said they stood for certain values like constitutionalism, commonsense, lower taxes, smaller government, and being conservative. Even though the Republican Party talked a good game, the problem was that they didn't always have the best follow-through. So, I thought that I could do something about that and I got involved. I started interning and working on a number of campaigns that were going on in the House and the Senate and I became the College Republican Chairman of my campus and then became the Executive Director of the Pennsylvania College Republicans. I also interned at a talk radio station in Philadelphia under Michael Smerconish and Glenn Beck.

After the 2006 campaign, I had an offer to go work at the Bush White House under Karl Rove. I said no thanks, as I had other opportunities on my mind at the time.

Now this is where my story becomes a little different. After I graduated college in 2007— instead of continuing to work in politics like many people do—I decided to do a study abroad program. Well, it started as a study-abroad, but then I got a job and stayed for a while. I spent two years in China and I lived in the city of Shanghai, working for the American Chamber of Commerce there. It was one of the most eye-opening experiences of my life. A lot of people ask me what living in China was like. I tell them how it was always very informative and educational, and I learned something new every day. I even got to make a movie with Jackie Chan and Jet Li - Google it!

But the thing that I learned the most while living overseas wasn't about China. It was about America. I firmly believe that nobody can actually understand the truth about the United States of America until you've spent a significant amount of time away from it. Once you visit another country and are out of the same daily routine of your regular life, out of your comfort zone, only then can you appreciate the vast differences between America and the rest of the world. Hipster trips for a few days here and there do not count. A week or more, at least. And lemme tell you, the rest of the world ain't like the United States. We've got something very special and unique in this country. They used to call it "American Exceptionalism." I never really understood exactly what that meant until I left America.

After I returned home from China, I went to work on other campaigns from 2008 to 2010, as well as with the David Horowitz Freedom Center. It was during that time that Barack Obama was elected President and the Tea Party revolution was born. I was very involved with it. If any of you don't know what the Tea Party is, you better wake up because guess what—you are living it right now. That's a pretty good segue to our next chapter, so I'll quit rambling and get on with it.

In 2010, I joined the US Navy. I first was enlisted and then was commissioned a reserve officer. I served multiple deployments overseas, to include a tour at Guantanamo Bay, Cuba. It gave me a huge respect for all of our armed services, and definitely influenced my attitude on the nature of armed conflict, and the sacrifice it means for those families who have lost a son or daughter wearing the uniform of our country.

2. TEA PARTY FOR TWO

The Tea Party revolution was the origin of the Populist movement in the United States, that helped get Donald Trump elected. The Tea Party revolution was begun as a response, not only to Barack Obama's election, but to the Republican Party, which many people felt had fallen short of the ideals for which the party stood. I can remember so many times that people would have Tea Party events and thousands of people would come together to talk about the constitution, free markets, free trade and what it was that they wanted their country to be, and that they were going to fight for their country.

The Tea Party movement got started as a response to a lot of the moves that Barack Obama was making not only in his first campaign but also his first hundred days in office. There was a reporter on CNBC who completely flipped out about the collusion between Barack Obama and Wall Street, between the federal government and Wall Street. He said live on CNBC that it's about time that we have a new Tea Party. Well, I would say that was one of the first political videos to go to viral and really one of the first times that people answered a call to action based on something that came around through the Internet.

In the Tea Party movement, people realized that they can use sites like Facebook and MeetUp to find like-minded people who had similar interests in preserving the United States of America the way it was and for fighting against the moneyed interests in Washington. The Tea Party was a force to be reckoned with and in 2010 they succeeded in taking back the House of Representatives for Republicans and contributed to one of the biggest landslides in US history. At that time, the House of Representatives was seen as a way to check Obama's policies because, at that point, Obama and the Democrats had all three parts of government. However, as we saw, once the Republican Party took back the House, they did little to stop Barack Obama over the next few years.

It was during the Tea Party revolution of 2010 that I worked for a candidate for lieutenant governor in Pennsylvania named Steve Johnson. Now, Steve Johnson didn't win his race. despite having the best deputy campaign manager in the world (and arguably the most handsome.)

Steve Johnson was an unlikely candidate for statewide office. He was a businessman and a veteran who served overseas in the Gulf War in the U.S. Army. He was not politically correct, was not ideological, but was seen as the man of the people. A complete outsider running against the insiders. We ran his entire campaign that way. A man of the people, who wasn't afraid to say the hard things that needed to be said, and to let people know the many problems that were going on both in our country and in the state of Pennsylvania. In that campaign, I pioneered many tools that I echoed in the 2016 campaign. You might call it the test run of some of the things that were to come. Foreshadowing. We had a large primary with over 10 different individuals running in it. We used tactics like coming up with nicknames for each candidate, like "Double-dipping Darryl," "Swearing Sam," and "Rusty Russ." We also made funny videos and memes that we shared on the Internet. We found that with these memes and very little budget, we were able to break through the mainstream media cycle and get our message across to the voters.

We got a lot of attention for what we did and a lot of people said that they were were very impressed with the way that we ran a campaign. They were very surprised that someone with no political experience could run a campaign that gotten that many votes in the entire state. The problem was that not enough people were on social media just yet and that we hadn't quite embraced the power of it, so it hadn't yet reached critical mass.

What we understood though, was that social media was a force to be reckoned with. A new revolution was coming in the way political campaigns were run. If enough people had seen our message through social media and using our ability to make persuasive arguments with the help of advertisements that were easy, quick, completely free, truth-telling, factual evidence of what was going on with our opponents, we would've won.

After 2010 I worked on another statewide campaign, another businessman outsider candidate, but PA wasn't ready yet. I found myself becoming disillusioned with politics and decided to try something else. I worked for CBS Radio for a stint, and then joined the US Navy. I supported worldwide fleet operations, OIF/OEF, and deployed to a number of places, including Guantanamo Bay, Cuba. I always said I wouldn't get back into politics unless it felt right. And then Donald Trump entered the race.

Donald Trump very early on saw the Tea Party as an important force in the American political spectrum. He saw that the Tea Party represented something different from the Republicans and the Democrats. The Tea Party represented something purer, closer to the ground, and closer to the heart of people. These are people that were motivated, not by money, power, or wealth, but by love of this country and the desire for a better life for themselves and their families. Donald Trump knew that these people would be very strong allies for him if he ever ran for office.

Looking at the movement very early on, Donald Trump began to talk about them on his Twitter account. He used to chastise the Republican Party elites for not listening to the Tea Party, for treating them as if they were not important, and for spending more time paying attention to the issues of the donor class rather than the middle class.

Donald Trump had a different idea. He found that the Tea Party, as well as himself, represented something completely different and completely new for American politics. He saw that the Tea Party was a nonpartisan movement aimed at making the country better than it currently was. He knew that deep down, every member of the Tea Party simply wanted to make America great again. That is why. in 2010 and 2011, Donald Trump began making many political statements and political observations, mainly through his Twitter account and other forms of media. He focused on criticism of Barack Obama, who he knew was a favorite target of the Tea Party. At this time, he also criticized Republican leaders for failing to stand up to Barack Obama. We found that this would become a hallmark of Donald Trump's campaign in 2016.

All of this activity made many speculate if Donald Trump would run for office in 2012 against Barack Obama. Donald Trump himself has said that if he'd run in 2012, he would've beaten Obama and held him to a one-term presidency. However, Donald Trump also frequently stated that he would only run if he did not feel there any other contenders or candidates who are up to the task. And so, in 2012, Donald Trump did what he normally did, endorsed the Republican candidate and donated heavily to the Republican cause.

In 2011, I attended the annual CPAC (Conservative Political Action Conference) in Washington, D.C. At one point, I was standing in the line at Starbucks in the lobby waiting for a coffee. I turned to hear a large commotion. Looking around, I saw a large group of men entering the lobby all clad in black suits. I couldn't tell what was going on. And then I heard a whisper start to go through the crowd, *it's him, he's here.* Looking across the sea of black suits, I could see one thing sort of floating above them; a smooth tapered-back swath of blonde hair. It was Donald Trump.

Donald Trump took the stage at CPAC, despite not having been invited or even being on the speaking schedule whatsoever. That didn't matter too much to Donald Trump. He wanted to speak, and so he walked up on stage and asked MC *would you mind if I have a few words?* He proceeded to give a speech about how immigration was changing the United States of America and that how we needed border security if we ever wanted to get our country back on the right track. He talked about the importance of trade deals, and how we were getting ripped off by other countries around the world. He gave a fiery speech and the entire room was on their feet applauding him. I remember thinking *wow, I wish this guy was running for President!*

3. YOU NEVER SEE A THIN PERSON DRINKING DIET COKE

It began with a tweet.

One of the most referenced exchanges from Donald Trump's Twitter account, prior to his announcement of his candidacy, was is in 2013 when he was juxtaposing Barack Obama's support for the drone assassination program with his lack of support for waterboarding. Trump was pointing out that it made no sense for someone to call waterboarding inhumane while assassination with a missile fired from a flying robot was permissible. Someone responded to Mr. Trump replying "why don't you run for President and fix everything?" and Trump responded "Be careful!"

Donald Trump understood very early on the power of social media, in particular, the power of Twitter. He knew that the way to win public opinion was to sway as many individuals as possible through mass communications. By getting his message out to as many people as possible he had a greater chance of winning the nomination and eventually the general election. This is true for any candidate of any race. However, in 2016, Trump was able to revolutionize the way in which social media had an influence on the campaign.

Trump was given a 5 minute pitch on what Twitter was back in 2009, and he immediately decided to sign up for the service. This is far earlier than most people were interested in Twitter. In 2009, Twitter had 30,000,000 monthly active users. By 2016, Twitter had over 300 million monthly active users. Trump realized early on that people would be interested in receiving a way to communicate directly with marketed brands and celebrities, and in his case, he was reportedly very eager to find an outlet that allowed him to communicate directly to the people. We can't know if he intended this from the start to be used politically rather than merely for business branding. But as the Trump candidacy has shown, perhaps those are more similar than we have been led to believe.

Traditionally, campaigns break down media into two categories: earned media and paid media. Paid media is the advertising that most people usually associate with campaigns. The advertising includes the positive candidate messages and the infamous negative ads. Many people often bemoan the fact that negative ads are used at all, but the basic reasoning among political consultants is that negative advertising works better, because people remember it more readily. Earned media is the term used by news media themselves covering the candidate in their efforts to achieve office. To this end, candidates hire communications directors, press secretaries, and cultivate relationships with the press in order to get their message across to the public. Typically, a candidate would not have the same type of reach as a regional publication or national news outlet. Therefore, the reasoning is that with earned media, a candidate can reach more voters. There is a secondary benefit to earned media, in that because it is not paid for by the candidate, it is supposed to be objective reporting and therefore more credible.

All of that changed in 2016.

Using Twitter, and eventually Facebook and Instagram, Trump was able to break through establishment barriers that would have been hard to crack at any other time in history for an outsider candidate. In doing so, he built his own grassroots network across the country that did not fall within the confines of any existing organization or institution like the NRA, the SEIU, or the AARP. Instead, Trump leapfrogged the normal series of checkmarks a Republican candidate would be expected to accomplish in a primary run: going to the right groups, raising money from the right people, getting the blessings of former presidents and presidential candidates - a process known colloquially as 'kissing the ring'. These groups then would turn over their vast resources and member lists to the candidate, which usually propels them to victory. Trump did none of the sort. Instead, he created his own community: The Trump Network. In early 2016, he suddenly saw his tweets go from around 100 retweets to regularly 2,000 or more. By the end of the campaign, Trump was regularly seeing 10,000 retweets with every tweet. He was able to effectively craft his message to the American people by seeing what resonated and what did not. In the same way, the people were able to 'vote with their tweets' and either reward the candidate or not, depending on the message. There has rarely been a more pure form of direct interaction between a candidate and the electorate. Time will tell what this direct democracy 'flattening' effect may have on Trump's presidency, but the American experiment in self-governance just got a whole lot more interesting!

For the uninitiated, Trump's twitter may seem like chaos. For the politicos used to polished, focus-grouped messaging from their candidate, Trump's twitter was downright offensive.

On Dec 9, 2015, the Washington Post (in a rare bout of journalistic objectivity) published an analysis of Trump's twitter account done by Paul Schwartzman and Jenna Johnson. Its key findings were:

• Trump delivers scores of promises, diatribes and insults at breakneck speed.
• He attacks a regular cast of villains, including undocumented immigrants, Muslims, the Democrat front-runner Hillary Clinton, his GOP rivals and the media.
• He keeps the narrative arc of each controversy alive with an endless stream of statements and an unwillingness to back down.

The analysis also showed how Trump's twitter is a real-time message tester. It's part of-the-moment, part incredibly deliberate. When a message doesn't work — like a joke about Bernie Sanders's hernia surgery that fell flat— Trump drops it and never looks back. In the volume of tweets he sends and speeches he gives, it gets buried in a day anyway. This type of A/B testing can cost hundreds of thousands when done from 5th Avenue consulting firms. Trump crowd-funded it for free. Paid campaign messaging strategists may be yet another business Trump proved is ineffective and useless and may soon be going the way of the dinosaur in the Internet era of political campaigning.

Trump also realized that his social media could, in turn, be used to generate earned media. In online lingo, he began trolling the mainstream media. The situation became almost a clear formula in the primaries. First, Trump would tweet something or say something that was over-the-top edgy, but with truth to it. The media would then breathlessly report this controversy, in their view, giving Trump hours and hours of free time. With each new uproar, millions of eyes and ears would be given to Trump and his message. The media and establishment politicians would call for Trump to end his campaign, he would refuse, and he would go up in the polls. From the beginning of his campaign through February 2016, Trump received almost $2 billion in free media attention. According to data from the Tyndall Report, which tracks nightly news content, through February 2016, Trump alone accounted for more than a quarter of all 2016 election coverage on the evening newscasts of NBC, CBS and ABC, more than all the Democratic campaigns combined. Observers have noted Trump's ability to garner constant mainstream media coverage almost at will.

In a January 2016 interview with CBS, Trump said of his campaign's plans to purchase advertising; "I think I'm probably wasting the money. But I'm $35 million under budget. Look, I was going to have $35 or 40 million spent by now. I haven't spent anything. I almost feel guilty … I'm leading by, as you all say, a lot. You can take the CBS poll. You can take any poll and I'm winning by a lot. I don't think I need the ads."

Here is a not-anywhere-near-comprehensive list of Trump "controversies" that were given endless coverage in the press:

- Megyn Kelly feud
- Rosie O'Donnell feud
- Barack Obama feud
- Trump University

- Trump University judge
- Trump's taxes
- Trump's Polish workers
- Eminent Domain
- Michelle Fields
- Buying his own books
- Using his own buildings
- Comments on illegal immigrants
- Comments on John McCain
- Comments on David Duke
- The taco bowl tweet
- The Corrupt Hillary Star Meme
- Comments on Khizr Khan
- Obama is the founder of ISIS and Hillary is their MVP (probably his best deliberate media troll)
- Various nicknames for his opponents (you know you know them all)

In addition to his millions of fans on Twitter and Facebook, no discussion of Trump's social media dominance could be complete without mentioning Reddit and the forum "The_Donald." At nearly 300,000 subscribers, the subreddit "/r/The_Donald" on Reddit has faced controversy since its inception, but was also the most popular group on the entire site for months. At one point, it had become so popular that the administrators of Reddit decided to censor them from the main Reddit homepage. This was due to it's intense engagement and active base, such that the entire home page was nothing but content from The_Donald. On July 27, 2016, Trump participated in an Ask Me Anything (AMA) on /r/The_Donald, answering thirteen questions from his supporters. The AMA broke the reddit site-wide record for most awards of "reddit gold" at 113, beating the previous record of 95.

Trump's online following's size, scope, and intensity was an early indication of the vast enthusiasm gap that would only grow between his supporters and the supporters of all other candidates. This would prove to be one of the critical factors that propelled him to victory in November.

It goes without saying that Trump far outpaced all candidates of both parties with his use of, and responsiveness to, social media. This alone is so key to his success in being elected that it was actually the cornerstone of his campaign. It is not the first time a candidate has won a race by embracing a new form of communication.

4 HOW DID WE END UP HERE?

Donald Trump's victory in 2016, and the movement which propelled him to victory, did not occur in a vacuum. The nomination of Donald Trump would likely have never occurred had things in the United States not gotten as bad as they had become. Several issues played major factors in the movement behind building up Donald Trump's presidential candidacy. These factors were largely unaddressed by both the Democrats and Republicans. The main factors would prove to be jobs, immigration, and security.

Working-class Americans by 2016 had not seen a real wage increase in nearly 20 years. That statistic alone would have been enough for any candidate who addressed it to easily win both the nomination of their party and the general election. In 1992, Bill Clinton's campaign famously used the message, "It's the economy, stupid." How this message was forgotten, let alone forgotten by the Clinton's themselves, will remain one of the biggest unanswered questions of the 2016 cycle.

As early as 1993, Donald Trump was on-record as being against NAFTA because it hurt the American worker. Apparently, when Bill Clinton said "It's the economy, stupid.", he wasn't talking about the American economy.

Donald Trump understood at that time that NAFTA aided other countries more than it aided the American people. He is on-record throughout the 1990's, 1980's and even the 1970's that he believed the United States trade policy should not be about goods but should focus on American currency and American workers first. Donald Trump took out a full-page advertisement in the New York Times in the 1980's railing against US trade policy with Japan and other countries. On an episode of Oprah, Trump was once asked if he would run for president, and he replied no, but that he was sick of seeing the United States getting ripped off.

So to hear American civil and government infrastructure have been crumbling for many decades from bridges falling apart, to Third-World-quality airports, to military hardware from the Vietnam war still found in service, as well as the shuttering of the American space program NASA, Americans felt that those in government with their hands on the rudder of the country were steering into dangerous waters.

While the Hillary Clinton campaign initially focused on touting her foreign policy experience, Donald Trump had already achieved a 40-year record of fighting to protect the American worker.

Keep that in mind the next time you are told that by electing Donald Trump, Americans voted against their self-interests.

The issue of immigration and illegal immigration has been written about extensively in many other publications. The key to understanding this issue is simply that from the 1970's until now, America has experienced the most drastic demographic and economic shift since her founding. While elites are quick to shut down discussion of this issue anytime, only one candidate was willing to discuss it openly and freely as an issue that Americans were facing.

Donald Trump did his research. Prior to the election, Mr. Trump asked Roger Stone and other operatives to conduct a research report for him. He asked him to listen to talk radio stations around the country. Local stations, talking about local issues. The purpose of the report was to find out if there were any issues that were being talked about in every corner of the nation. What issue was affecting Americans in the Northeast, Midwest, the South and the West? The main issue that was found was that of illegal immigration.

Americans were told under several administrations that they should not worry about illegal immigration, that it wasn't dangerous to the United States, that it wasn't a danger to their families, that it wasn't a danger to their jobs and that it was being taken care of by big brother.

The American people were not convinced.

The crime wave of violence by illegal immigrants was completely covered up by the mainstream media. These murders and rapes were treated as unconnected to each other and separate from any national trend. The plague of illegal narcotics and drug related violence pouring across the border into the United States was similarly covered up by mainstream outlets. It has been called a Border War by Customs and Border Protection agents. Donald Trump was the only one that discussed the issue with a wide audience.

While the mainstream media was gleeful to discuss violence involving firearms, they have been remiss to discuss the root causes of such violence, namely the narcotics trade. Quite possibly, one of the biggest unreported stories in America is human trafficking, which brings many individuals into the

United States, not as legal immigrants, but into a shadowy form of modern slavery. Many of these trafficking victims are women and children, and are subject to sexual abuse. The media refuses to report it. Donald Trump famously crystallized these issues into a tangible policy: The Wall.

Related to the violence perpetuated by illegal immigrants, was the string of domestic terrorist attacks carried out by adherence to radical Islam within the United States. While the United States under President Obama was attempting to use proxies to defeat ISIS overseas, the terrorists were using propaganda and meme warfare to gain recruits in the United States and urge them to carry out attacks on unsuspecting Americans. From the Fort Hood shooting to the Boston bombing, to the Chattanooga attack, to the Orlando Pulse Nightclub attack, and more, it seemed as though nothing was being done to protect the homeland.

The migrants from the Middle East, who were brought into both Europe and the United States, also caused a shock to the system for many ordinary Americans. To many, the rationale for bringing in hundreds of thousands of unvetted and potentially dangerous individuals just did not make sense. And it made people fear for the lives of their children. These issues were crystallized into the policies of extreme vetting of immigrants and working with new allies to defeat ISIS abroad.

By the time Donald Trump began his exploratory committee for the presidency, he had already had an interesting past in politics. He had never been an ideological Democrat or Republican. Mr. Trump changed from one party to the other several times, and even once briefly ran for president as an independent candidate in 2000. Early on, there were rumors that Trump would run as an Independent or even a Democrat in 2016. What Donald Trump set out to do was to campaign as a pragmatic American Nationalist candidate. He was not attempting to win the favor of the ideological elites on either side of the aisle. He knew that to play to only one extreme would alienate the vast majority.

Now, for those of you who didn't get it the first time around, is the meaning of, and the reason for the success of: *Make America Great Again.*

5 THE HERO WE NEED

Why Donald Trump in the first place? Donald Trump is a man who had never been elected to an office in his entire life. Donald Trump does not have experience in government. Donald Trump has a sordid history that has played out across tabloid magazines and newspaper stands and supermarket aisles for the past 30 years. So it came as a huge surprise that so many of the American people would get behind such a man to lead them at a time when America was in need of a great leader.

Many pundits and experts thought that the only reason the Republican Party had lost in 2008 and 2012 was that Barack Obama was so popular. They thought that all the Republicans needed to do was elect a candidate that was similar to Barack Obama, but had more Republican values. They also thought that people wanted to see a candidate who had a squeaky clean exterior. They thought that the American people wanted to choose someone seen as upright, upstanding, and 100% wholesome.

Donald Trump is an antihero. Donald Trump does not fit the mold of most American presidents and certainly not the mold of most Republican candidates.

However, the rise of the antihero has been played out in American cinema and American media since about 1999. From Tony Soprano, Frank Underwood, Walter White, Tyrion Lannister, The Dark Knight, and Don Draper, America is currently in the midst of a rise in the popularity of antihero drama.

Antiheroes were also popular in the past, just look at Dirty Harry, the Man with No Name, or Han Solo. These characters were not necessarily traditional heroes, but have enjoyed great popularity in the past as well. The outlaw rogue, the cowboy, the pirate, the hard-

boiled detective are all common examples of antiheroes.

The "antihero" (also known as the flawed hero) is a common character archetype for the protagonist that has been around since the comedies and tragedies of Greek theater. Unlike the traditional hero who is morally upright and steadfast, the anti-hero usually has a flawed moral character. The moral compromises he or she makes can often be seen as the unpleasant means to an appropriately desired end—such as breaking a finger to get answers—whatever it takes for the protagonist to come to justice. Other times, however, the moral flaws can also be personality flaws.

Why are we drawn to antiheroes? And why are we drawn to antiheroes now? Antiheroes typically have a stronger moral complexity than traditional heroes. But the traditional hero is a two dimensional character. The traditional hero does the right thing because it's the right thing. The antihero has a complex series of decisions and a complex series of emotions that lead to them choosing to be heroic. This complex moral decision-making is much more realistic and much more relatable to everyday people than the traditional superhero. It is easier to relate to Batman than to Superman.

The antihero offers a way to liberate us. The antihero is typically portrayed as antisocial. Their behavior and actions are seen as contrary to social norms and possibly contrary to the unwritten code of conduct which all traditional heroes follow. The antihero does not care about these things. The antihero cares about one thing: getting the job done. The antihero isn't afraid to do what it takes to take care of business. In a way, an antihero can be seen as almost outside of society, not constrained by society, and ultimately able to affect change in society on a great scale because of their willingness to not play by society's rules. In the past, antiheroes received much acclaim, with a rise in popularity following World War II and the Great Depression. It was a time when many American soldiers had just returned from overseas, participating in some of the most violent acts and having to grow up in an extremely hard time when families had to make tough choices in order to survive. Following September 11, 2001, there have been wars in Iraq, Afghanistan, and around the world in the ensuing 15 years. This has been coupled with a rise in terrorist attacks in the United States, as well as mounting pressures from criminal illegal-aliens, domestic disturbances, struggling economy, and drastic changes in the workforce. Many American families had been living through very hard times by 2016. It was into this situation that Donald Trump began his run for the presidency.

There are three things every candidate needs in order to win an election:

They need to be the **right person**, at the **right place**, at the **right time**. Had Donald Trump run for president during the early 2000's or back in the 90's, he may not have received the same success as he did in 2016.

There is a story that while he was exploring the possibility of running in 2015, his wife, Melania, came to him one day and pointed out the riots going on in the streets of Baltimore (which I reported from live).

Seeing them, she remarked, "If you run now, you will win."

"Why do you say that?" Mr. Trump replied.

"Because something has changed," Melania said. "America is ready for you."

6 THE ANNOUNCEMENT

From the moment Donald Trump threw his hat into the ring in the Republican primary, he was the main event. He descended down the escalator in front of a waterfall in the lavish lobby of a building he built that bore his name on the exterior. The moment was immediately iconic, owing to Trump's unique flair for theatricality. No other candidate on either side of the race garnered more public interest, more supporter enthusiasm, and more head-scratching from the members of the mainstream media. Trump was immediately opposed as a demagogue. Many thought his announcement was just a PR stunt, or, as many believed, even a Hillary Clinton planted candidate, intended to disrupt the expansive Republican field and exploit a hard-fought primary to the eventual benefit of Hillary in November.

On June 16, 2015, Donald Trump shocked America and the world by announcing that he would run for President of the United States. In a 51-minute speech given without notes, teleprompters, or cue cards, he ran through a laundry list of problems facing America.

Immigration. Debt. National security. Terrorism. Unemployment. Trade balance. Outsourcing jobs. Education. Obamacare. The 2nd Amendment. Corruption within Washington DC from both parties.

It had been a long time since Americans had heard anyone speak to them like that. Real talk. Simple numbers. Issues that the majority of Americans talk about, but rarely are heard as talking points from the Democrat or Republican Parties. Trump was brash, loud, in-your-face, and pulled no punches.

From the start, many Americans immediately turned to hear what the famous billionaire had to say. What they heard was abrasive, counter-narrative and bold. To many of them, it represented a new way of thinking about politics, and about governance. Trump re-framed the outlook of all of American government with that one speech, and in many ways, re-framed the entire campaign. For years, candidates had argued about cold metrics, esoteric ideals, or policies to deal with countries in far-flung corners of the world that most Americans would never travel to or be affected by personally.

Trump deftly changed the entire conversation from the abstract to the concrete. His very first statement was:

"Our country is in serious trouble. We don't have victories anymore. When was the last time anybody saw us beating, let's say, China in a trade deal? They kill us. I beat China all the time. All the time. When did we beat Japan at anything? They send their cars over by the millions, and what do we do? When was the last time you saw a Chevrolet in Tokyo? It doesn't exist, folks. They beat us all the time. When do we beat Mexico at the border? They're laughing at us."

It is interesting to note that from that moment on, not a single other candidate in the primary or general ever challenged Trump on this statement. None of them had any response. The reason was simple; they did not realize that the American voter had now shifted their definition of what a president's job was. Bush campaigned on the promise of security. Obama campaigned on the promise of hope. Trump, instead, re-framed the debate to one of America's standing in the world relative to other countries, and by extension, the American people's standing economically and socially. Instead of platitudes about America being the greatest country in the world, Trump gained immediate credibility with voters by acknowledging the hard truths that both of the major parties had largely ignored or kicked down the road.

At the time, many in the media and the establishment mocked Trump as a sideshow attraction to their civilized croquet match of an election. Trump drove a Sherman tank through their parade grounds, waving the largest America flag he could find. Americans tuned in.

He may not have won their support yet, but he had won their attention.

7 HOW TRUMP WON THE PRIMARIES

At first, people were not sure what to think when Donald Trump entered an already packed field of Republicans on June 16, 2015. The field included the likes of Jeb Bush, Ted Cruz, Marco Rubio, John Kasich, and Ben Carson among others. The RNC had already announced that there would be twelve debates and nine forums. The "experts" were anticipating Jeb Bush to breeze through the field, as Americans were already familiar with his name, without consideration for the American people's general lack of interest in political dynasties. Then Jeb would inevitably face Hillary for the presidency in a Bush vs Clinton showdown of epic proportions. The experts were wrong. From the very first debate it was clear, the 2016 presidential election would be atypical in every aspect. Expecting the unexpected became the norm. Donald Trump transformed the presidential primaries from a humdrum, phoned-in affair into a no-holds-barred free-for-all rollercoaster never before seen in American politics. Much has been made of the excess time given to Mr. Trump at the debates, but let's face it, if other candidates wanted more time they should have been more interesting. And no, Rand, the hair doesn't count.

The first debate was held on August 6, 2015, almost 2 months after Trump announced his bid. The debate was held in Quicken Loans Arena in Cleveland Ohio, the same arena that the Republican National Convention would be held a year or so later. Fox News and Facebook hosted the debate that would include a field of ten hopeful candidates such as Ted Cruz, Ben Carson, Chris Christie, Jeb Bush, Mike Huckabee, John

Kasich, Rand Paul, Marco Rubio, Scott Walker, and Trump himself. The moderators were Bret Baeir, Megyn Kelly, and Chris Wallace. Trump was predictably the star of the show. Right from the start, he voiced his stance that he could not pledge to support the eventual nominee; he was the only candidate to say this. Throughout the night, Trump was given the most time to speak, 10 minutes and 32 seconds, over 2 minutes more than Jeb Bush, the candidate with the 2nd most time to speak. The debate itself was viewed by 24 million people, the most watched presidential debate in history. It was also the highest rated non-sports telecast in cable television history.

In the primetime debate, frontrunner Donald Trump's overall performance was criticized as rude and erratic by many pundits, while others said his comments were popular and his criticisms were overdue, including his criticism of Bush's description of illegal immigration as an "act of love". Cruz, Rubio, Christie and Huckabee received praise. Notable conflicts between candidates included Paul vs. Christie over the NSA surveillance program, Paul vs. Trump on the latter's possible third-party run, Paul vs. Trump on healthcare, and Christie vs. Huckabee on the issue of welfare reform. Trump also clashed with two of the moderators – Kelly and Wallace – on the issue of sexism with Kelly, and on the issue of illegal immigration with Wallace. Their specific point of contention was Trump's claims that the Mexican government was deliberately sending criminals into America illegally. While Megyn Kelly began her feud with Trump that night, she would eventually be reduced to irrelevance by her shrill attacks, and excommunicated to NBC News. Americans tuned in to watch Donald Trump, and when they did, they turned to his side. Trump spoke to them in the way they had always wanted to be addressed by a leader – honestly.

8 LOW ENERGY JEB!

In 2013, the GOP Establishment stacked the deck for Jeb Bush's nomination. If you want all the details of this, you have to go to the Conservative Treehouse and read "The GOP Roadmap" by the enigmatic and rarely-incorrect Sundance. The TLDR (too long, didn't read) version is, the GOP establishment knew that they would need to devise a strategy to elect Jeb Bush with only around 15 – 25% of the primary vote, depending on the state, and carry him through the first nine calendar primary races. This approach made winning a simple matter of math, not ideology or politics. "The sum of the Jeb Bush vote must be greater than any individual part within the Not-Jeb vote." That approach would have guaranteed a Jeb victory with far less support than a majority or even a strong plurality in any state. This is why many states, notably Florida, were changed to winner-take-all delegate states. Even if Jeb only won 15% of the vote, if the next candidate only won 14%, Jeb would still collect all the delegates. To this end, the GOP then propped up numerous candidates (totaling 17 in all) in an effort to strategically split the Republican primary vote and hand the nomination to Jeb. This was accomplished via Super-PAC financing, inter-party alignment, money and state establishment party support. As Sundance noted, in order for this to succeed, each faction within Not-Jeb needed multiple options for voters. Evangelicals (Santorum, Huckabee), Tea Partiers, fiscal conservatives, Libertarians, Moderates, along with voters who might vote based on race (Carson), and/or gender (Fiorina) preferences. These could all be smaller fractures inside Non-Jeb. Then, these candidates would be like Pac-Man gobbling up delegate votes from more conservative candidates, and planning to drop them back off in the bucket of Jeb Bush after endorsement at specific dates. Then, the election would be a boring affair of Jeb versus Hillary, which many rightly saw as two sides of the same coin.

Enter Donald John Trump.

Trump knew well about the GOP establishment plans for Jeb, and therefore made Jeb his initial target. Trump used bombastic comments early on towards Jeb, to set the tone for who was going lead the Republican Party. Trump's tone embodied a movement that would fight against political correctness, and upheld truth as an ideal, regardless of how acceptable it was. Trump knew early on that the deck was stacked so that Jeb would easily walk to the nomination. The RNC, as early as 2014, had changed the rules in the various state primaries to favor Jeb, and then used establishment money to prop up candidates that would split key voting blocs, such as social conservatives. The pathway to the nomination was only through Jeb Bush. Rather than focus on any of the lower-tier candidates, Trump instead targeted the frontrunner. On the night of December 15, 2015 at the 5th GOP debate (my birthday!), hosted by

CNN, Trump started the fire with, "Honestly, I think Jeb is a very nice person, but we need tough people.… Jeb said when they come across the Southern border, they come as an act of love." Jeb proceeded to intercede, interrupting Trump, leading to Trump instantly shutting him down, "Am I talking or are you talking?" Bush would not back down; he kept attempting to butt in. "Are you going to apologize? No!" Trump joked, as the audience cheered him on. They saw how hard Trump was fighting, and responded to it with approval.

Jeb momentarily ceased his meaningless jibes, but then a few moments later he tried a cringeworthy joke, "a little taste of your medicine there." Jeb said with a schoolboy smirk. Trump would then finish him with, "I know you tried to build up your energy there Jeb, but it's not working".

A look of regret and embarrassment quickly spread across Jeb's face as the audience responded to Trump's wit and charisma with cheers and laughter. Jeb intelligently waited patiently this time for his turn to speak, where he then spouted, "Donald, you're not gonna be able to insult your way to the presidency. That's not gonna happen. And I do have the strength." Jeb said that, but upon looking at his face it was clear he didn't believe it himself. This moment would go on to be talked about for weeks. Saturday Night Live even did a spoof on this, which was quite funny. The term 'Low Energy Jeb' caught on, and he never lived it down. Coupled with the albatross already around his neck from his last name, his primary chances were a goner.

Trump however, was not finished, Jeb still had a few lessons to be learned. Jeb gathered up what little energy he had left and fired at Trump, this time questioning his toughness. "This is a tough business" Jeb said, to which Trump mocked him by saying, "Oh yeah, you're a real tough guy, Jeb." To which Jeb replied with the same, boring, comeback line of, "You're never gonna be able to insult your way to the presidency". Trump replied, "Well I'm at 42 and your at 3, so far I'm doing better" (referring to voting percentages). When Jeb said "My mother is one of the strongest people I know," Trump quipped, "Well, maybe she should be running."

The moderators finally interrupted the verbal back and forth, but the damage was done to Jeb. The American voters only saw a weak, cowering man that could not stand up to Donald Trump. How could he possibly handle debating Hillary Clinton, Russia, Iran, ISIS, or leading the country as the Commander-in-Chief? What voters want to see first and foremost in a leader is strength. Trump understood this. Jeb did not.

Jeb! Bush suspended his campaign on February 20th, 2016, after poor showings in early states and failing to win any delegates in the South Carolina primary.

Few understood the impact of Trump so quickly defeating a member of the Bush Family, one of America's first families in politics, akin to a sort of American royalty. The blame was mostly laid on Jeb, or on the Bushes in general for "dynasty-fatigue" after two presidents so recently in the voter's recent memory. Instead, House Bush was much more formidable than House Clinton in 2016, as Clinton had been defeated before by Obama and his alignment with Ted Kennedy and his wing of the Democrat establishment. If Trump could defeat the Bush Family so easily, why did people ever think he would have trouble with the Clintons?

9 LIL MARCO

(Senator Marco Rubio sitting in a chair)

During the February 2016 CNN debate in Houston, Texas, Trump slammed "Lil Marco" Rubio for his Senate voting record. Rubio attempted to counter-assault Trump's alleged use of illegal Polish labor for many of his projects. "You're only person on this stage that has ever been fined for hiring people to work on your projects illegally," Rubio said of Trump. "You hired some workers from Poland—" Trump quickly shut Rubio down, "No, no, I'm the only one on the stage that's hired people. You haven't hired anybody." The crowd received this with laughter, and applause. The crowd's response was significant – they were simply resonating with Trump's humor and wit much more than the policies that the other contenders were laying out. With the title, "Lil Marco" – a linguistic kill shot according to Scott Adams, Trump was able to effectively dismiss and mock Senator Rubio via an extremely effective means. Trump turned Rubio into a meme. Instantly, Reddit found an old picture of Rubio in a big chair, and the meme went viral across social media. Photoshoppers began shrinking Rubio in images and having him walk off stage as Trump stood triumphantly at the stand. Soon thereafter, NJ Governor Chris Christie threw a strong attack at Rubio, picking up on the fact that Rubio constantly repeated the same attack line "we must dispel this notion" again and again, as if by rote. Robo-Rubio became the next meme, mocking Rubio as a cookie-cutter Republican politician akin to a wind-up toy that could be programmed to repeat any line and march in any direction he was told.

The Florida Republican primary was held on March 15, 2016. Florida was supposed to be the primary that gave the nomination to Jeb. Instead, with Jeb already withdrawn, Florida became the end of Lil Marco. Rubio, the sitting Senator of Florida, failed to win a single delegate in the state, as Trump took home 46% of the vote, and won all 99 delegates at stake. According to media exit polls taken that day, Trump won in a sweep of all age groups, income levels, and education levels.

For whites without a college degree, Trump won 54-22 over Rubio. Trump won with born-again and Evangelical Christians 46-24, Protestants 45-24, and Catholics 50-33. Trump not only won 100% of the delegates, he won every county in Florida, except for Miami-Dade.

In their analysis of Rubio's quickly-ended campaign, the NY Times wrote that Rubio failed to read the "mood" of the electorate, overlooking the deeply dissatisfied and angry sentiment many had about the Republican Party and government in general. The resulting image of Florida counties won with only one colored-in for Rubio prompted the meme that Rubio won 'just the tip.'

Whatever that means.

10 BENJI CARSON

      Trump's defeat of Ben Carson's campaign was the swiftest of them all, however so was his enlisting Ben Carson as an extremely useful ally. He effectively used Ben Carson's own book against him. In his book, Carson described glimpses of himself during his adolescent past as angry, nihilistic, and directionless. He described one particular incident in detail, in which he attempted to stab a classmate. Carson himself said he could have very easily killed this classmate had he not been restrained. Carson later used this example to explain how far he had come in building his patience and maturity. Trump wasn't buying it, and brought up these issues at debates. Trump claimed that Ben Carson has the signs of a someone with a pathological temper. Trump then went on to compare Carson's rage to the likes of a child molester, "That's a big problem; you don't cure that ... as an example: child molesting. You don't cure these people. You don't cure a child molester.

There's no cure for it. Pathological, there's no cure for that." Now comparing Carson to a child molester may have been a bit of a stretch, but Trump's damage to the Carson campaign was detrimental. Trump's remarks and Carson's inability to stay awake on the debate stage promptly ceased any momentum Carson's campaign had.

Significantly, Ben Carson then met with Trump in Florida, at Mar-a-Lago. Carson, while not a viable presidential candidate, did have a significant following, as well as a level of credibility with many voters due to his past career as an internationally-renowned neurosurgeon. As well, Carson represented someone who did not gain his following through the establishment GOP or the conservative movement. He was an outsider, like Trump. His endorsement would be a substantial boost to Trump as well as with Carson being a black American, to help fight back against lingering attacks on Trump from the left and the right as a racist due to his illegal immigration views. On March 11, 2016, Ben Carson threw his support behind Donald Trump, saying the two men had "buried the hatchet" and praising him as a "voice of the people to be heard." Carson also began the push to show other doubters that the over-the-top showman Trump of big rallies and reality TV was quite different from the tenor of the man in person.

Carson said, "Some people have gotten the impression that Donald Trump is this person who is not malleable, who does not have the ability to listen, and to take information in and make wise decisions. And that's not true. "He's much more cerebral than that."

From early on, Trump knew that the key to victory was to secure a base and then expand his coalition. Every opponent who faced Trump in 2016, including Hillary Clinton, seemed to forget this simple fact:

Politics is addition, not subtraction.

11 LYIN TED

The final challenger of any standing to Donald Trump, as the primary entered the summer, was Senator Ted Cruz of Texas. A Cuban born in Calgary, Cruz was one of the first to enter the race, announcing in March of 2015. Initially he was not considered to be a front runner, but he quickly gained popularity. Cruz's supporters were mainly evangelical Christians and constitutional conservatives. He had earned a strong following from the Tea Party during his first race in 2012, and retained much of his support base in those circles.

In full disclosure, I will state that shortly after

his announcement, representatives of the Cruz campaign reached out to me to recruit me for his run. They had known me from previous campaigns in Pennsylvania, and were looking for someone to help his campaign in the Northeast/Mid-Atlantic for field operations. Cruz' campaign hired many experienced political operatives, people who knew the system well. At the time, Donald Trump was rumored to be considering a run, but it would be several months still before he would come down the escalator. Still, I decided to decline to join with Cruz. I wrote a note back to the Cruz camp that I appreciated the offer, but that I thought Cruz could do a much better job as Senator from Texas than running nationally for president. The idea of jumping on a presidential campaign was not interesting to me unless it was for someone I really supported, and for someone I really thought could win against Hillary Clinton. Ted is great on policy, and knows the law extremely well, but I just didn't think he had what it took to win the presidency.

Cruz' big showing came with the first caucus, held in Iowa, on February 1st , 2016. Cruz won the state, but employed dirty tactics to do so. During the course of the caucus day, Ben Carson, who was polling well with evangelical voters in Iowa, made a comment in an interview that following the caucus, he would be returning to his home in Florida. The Cruz camp jumped on these comments, claiming Carson had meant he was dropping out of the race. While voting was still taking place, the Cruz campaign sent out emails to Republicans that Carson was dropping from the primary. At many of the precincts, information was disseminated that Carson was suspending his campaign, that he had dropped out, and anybody who was planning to vote for him was wasting their vote and, therefore, they should reconsider Cruz. After the massive deception campaign, Cruz shocked Republican voters as he won Iowa, which completely contradicted the amount of support Trump had throughout the country in national polls. However the false momentum did not last, and in the remaining span up until Super Tuesday, Cruz finished 3rd in South Carolina and New Hampshire, losing both to Donald Trump.

On the eve of Super Tuesday, Cruz was considered to be Trump's main, and perhaps only likely contender. His support among evangelical Christians was something that Trump could not yet match or win over. Cruz ended up winning three states on Super Tuesday - Alaska, Oklahoma, and his home state of Texas. Cruz would go onto win twelve total states before suspending his campaign after losing the so-called "firewall state" of Indiana to Trump.

Now, conventional political wisdom would say that the most conservative candidate would win the Republican primary and then tack to the middle for the general. However, Ted Cruz didn't win at all. Cruz is a Harvard graduate with strong ties to the Bush family, Karl Rove, and Goldman Sachs where his wife is a Vice President. Like Trump, Cruz spoke to the American people clearly with promises to do away with "progressive agendas" and give America back to the

American people. Cruz did not have controversial comments about John McCain or Megyn Kelly, and his family life of a wife and two daughters was tailor-made for the political mold. So, why would Republican voters choose Trump over him?

Because The Internet.

Ted Cruz was memed out of reality relentlessly on the social media, with a campaign of mockery leveled at him that seemingly no other politician in history has undergone. They mocked his appearance as 'creepy' and played old high school videos of Cruz declaring he would take over the world. They created zoomed-in gifs of lip flecks that appeared as Ted was speaking. Someone even created a Twitter account called 'TedCruzLipThing'. Social media found cut footage of Cruz trying to have his kids read a written script in a political ad, and found him acting extremely strangely in it – and ran it over and over and over. National Enquirer ran a piece alleging Cruz of having affairs with numerous former staffers, as well as a police report suggesting his wife at one point had contemplated suicide. There were also photos distributed that placed Ted Cruz' father, who had been born in Cuba, in the company of Lee Harvey Oswald shortly before the assassination of JFK. Donald Trump himself infamously commented on these, to much complaining in the media. Trump also raised the question of Cruz' Constitutional eligibility for the presidency, having been born a Canadian citizen. Cruz only renounced his Canadian citizenship shortly before his run for US president.

Perhaps the death knell for Cruz was just prior to the Indiana Primary, referring to a basketball hoop as a "basketball ring" – political suicide in the Hoosier State, a devastating gaffe that was played repeatedly on late-night TV, with many noting that basketball is not quite as popular in Canada, where Ted Cruz was born.

The one meme that ruled them all for the internet was Ted Cruz as the Zodiac Killer. This meme broke out from political circles and entered the young, mainstream, sarcastic-to-the-bone meme culture. If you aren't familiar with the Zodiac Killer, I shall inform you. During the 1960s and 70s, a serial killer plagued Northern California. The killer went by the pseudonym, "The Zodiac Killer" after he routinely wrote to the local newspapers, toying them with clues and puzzles, some

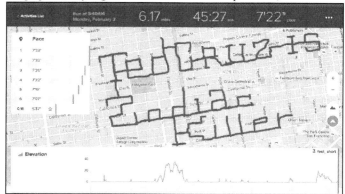

using Zodiac symbols. What also made The Zodiac Killer one of the most notorious and ominous killers ever, is that to this day, his identity is a mystery. What does this have to do with Ted Cruz? In March of 2013, the Twitter account, *@RedPillAmerica* tweeted, "#CPAC Alert: Ted Cruz is speaking!! His speech is titled: 'This is The Zodiac Speaking'" The tweet had little impact then, only racking up 200 or so retweets, but once the 2016 campaign kicked off in full steam, this "meme" took on a new life never seen before.

During the CBS debate, CBS included a Twitter trend tracker, in which the most popular tags on Twitter would show up on the bottom of the screen in the form of a ticker. Twitter user, @Vrunt tweeted several times to his followers, urging them to ask the question, "Is Ted Cruz the Zodiac Killer?" @Vrunt's tactic worked; the question reached the number one spot on the ticker, and the meme had taken full life, broadcasted to millions on live, national television.

This birthed the appearance of Ted Cruz Was The Zodiac Killer t-shirts, and a daily supply of fresh memes purporting to "prove" how Cruz was the killer – for example: "Ted Cruz was born in CALGARY. The Zodiac Killer's first two victims were CAL and GARY." On April 30th, 2016, comedian Larry Willmore repeatedly referred to Ted Cruz as the "Zodiac Killer" during his closing act at the White House Correspondents' Dinner. On May 2, YahooNews asked Ted Cruz's wife a theory about the jokes, and she replied, "Well, I've been married to him for 15 years, and I know pretty well who he is, so it doesn't bother me at all." Naturally, trolls took this as a tacit confession that only confirmed he was, in fact, the Zodiac Killer. The fact that Ted Cruz was born well after the killings took place only served to fuel the trolls even more.

A PPP (Public Policy Polling) poll taken before the primary found that 38% of Florida voters thought that there was a possibility that Ted Cruz very may well be the Zodiac Killer. The 21st century has proven that the Internet can make or break a career, and this case, it played a small part in derailing Ted Cruz's presidential campaign.

http://knowyourmeme.com/memes/ted-cruz-zodiac-killer

The internet supplied the stake for Ted Cruz, and Trump drove it deep into his heart. As Cruz became his final opponent, Trump zeroed in on him. The most prominent attack Trump used was his famous: "Lyin Ted!". This phrase is required to be shouted, so please take note if you ever say it out loud or if you ever should meet Ted Cruz on the street, as Baked Alaska once did at the RNC. Why did this phrase stick? Ted Cruz simply had a terrible habit of outright lying in speeches and debates. He lied so much you'd think he was a Clinton. He lied about Ben Carson dropping out of the race. He lied about Trump supporting Obamacare. He lied about taxes, guns, immigration, even the war on terror. At one point, he took to making up completely fictitious Trump quotes, such as stating "A couple of debates ago, Donald Trump said if you don't support socialized health care, you're heartless." A review of debates showed that Donald Trump made no statement even remotely close to this.

The candidates' wives also came into the crosshairs of mud-slinging as the Cruz camp used a racy photo from Melania Trump's modeling days in an attack ad. Trump fired back in a tweet, ominously threatening to "spill the beans" on Cruz's wife. Trump also retweeted a picture of his Slavic supermodel wife next to Heidi Cruz.

Following Cruz' withdrawal from the race, he was given a chance to speak at the Republican National Convention. At the event, after Trump had duly won the nomination, Cruz got up to speak. I was sitting in the room. The Senator rambled for several minutes before undercutting Trump as the candidate. Cruz urged voters to vote their conscience, implying that Trump may not be the best pick. I've never seen anyone misread a room as badly as Cruz did. The RNC delegate crowd may not have been completely on board with Trump going into the convention, but by the time Cruz spoke on Day Three, everyone had spent 72 hours being excited about Trump's prospects of defeating Hillary, and his rockstar appeal. The whole event was called Trumpfest by many. When Ted Cruz threw Trump under the bus at the RNC,

I honestly thought at one point the crowd was going to rush the stage. The only thing I can compare it to would be a mosh pit at a Rammstein concert. Reportedly, Heidi Cruz had to be escorted out of the area. Just as things began to turn ugly, Trump himself stepped out from the wings on the side of the stage, smiling. The crowd burst into applause. I have always remembered how Trump carefully orchestrated that moment, and how he was standing by watching the entire thing unfold. Donald Trump always uses public shaming as a tactic against his enemies. Always. Tywin Lannister would be proud.

12 THE PENNSYLVANIA PRIMARY

While most political operatives and grassroots activists were embroiled in a pitched battle for the Republican Primary in early 2016, I was not one of them. Normally, I would be right there in the trenches. Instead, I found myself overseas for work courtesy of the US Navy, sitting on the sidelines, catching up with the rollercoaster news and events of the day while sitting in front of a computer screen thousands of miles away from the United States.

It's a testament to the power of social media, YouTube, and livestreaming that I was able to be kept up-to-date as fast as possible with all the latest happenings from so far away. For those following me on social media, I am sure most people thought I was right home in the United States. I never posted anything about where I was or what I was doing. Work and personal life stay separate. And this time, it was personal (always wanted to say that).

Anyway, with Wi-Fi calling on the iPhone's FaceTime Audio, I was able to use my spare time after work to call friends and operatives all the way back home in Pennsylvania who I found were also supporting Trump. It was an extremely rough time for early Trump supporters. We would get emails and messages from powerful forces in the Republican establishment telling us that if we continued supporting Trump, we would find ourselves blacklisted and "never be able to work in politics again."

I've never been one to give in to strong-arm tactics. Or, any tactics, for that matter. When you tell me I can't do something, it only makes me want to do it a hundred times more. So, you can imagine the effect all of those hardball power-play moves had on me. I decided that if I couldn't volunteer for Donald Trump in person, I would do the next best thing, and in my spare time, I would become a digital volunteer. Little did I know where that would lead.

Digital volunteerism played a huge part in the primary and the general in 2016. Our ammunition was memes, videos, pictures, and positive support for Mr. Trump and the Make America Great Again agenda. We were the rebels. One thing I liked to do was do song parodies but change the words to make them about Trump. My apologies to Chuck Berry, but I still like my acoustic rendition of "Go Go! Go Donnie Go…Donnie. J Trump" – which is good because, as we all know, the internet never forgets.

The difference was, I had been a campaign field director and manager on 10 different campaigns in Pennsylvania. While each candidate is different, and each race is different, political warfare always uses the same tactics. I knew what needed to be done to win PA for Donald Trump.

Understand the rules of the race better than anyone else.

I read every law and statute about presidential primaries in PA for the Republican Party. It was confusing, and it was a lot to process, but it was doable. Three delegates would be selected for each congressional district in PA. Those delegates, unlike other states, would not be required to 'pledge' to support any specific presidential candidate and would travel to the overall convention in Cleveland as independent voters, in a sense. The answer there was simple – find out which delegates supported Trump, and promote those in each district. I organized press and media interviews for pro-Trump delegates in Philadelphia, Harrisburg, Pittsburgh, and across the state. I also got unpledged delegates to publicly endorse Donald Trump.

Mobilize and organize the troops

I reached out to the Trump campaign directly to find out exactly what they needed and where they needed it. I enlisted my own network of personal contacts, called through every single contact in my phone that was in or even near the Commonwealth of Pennsylvania, and then went public on the super-popular subreddit, "The_Donald" to ask for volunteer poll workers to come out on Election Day. I'll talk about this site in greater detail elsewhere in the book, but wow, is all I can say. Needless to say, they turned out for us like none other. Between the groundswell of support from the PA grassroots, and people I'd never met before on The_Donald, I was able to enlist poll workers from all over the East Coast to travel to key districts in PA on Primary Day. We had volunteers from six states and DC, in all. I spent a lot of sleepless nights messaging, emailing, and even talking on the phone with interested volunteers. The thing that struck me the most about these Trump volunteers was that not a single one of them asked for anything in return for their labors. All they wanted was for Mr. Trump to win, reward in itself.

(Meme I posted all over social media – with contact info redacted!)

Working with the Trump campaign, we developed and maintained a list of pro-Trump PA delegates for dissemination via social media, email, and plain old text message. At first, we maintained a public Google document with the names of each delegate, and which district, and who they were supporting. This was disseminated as well, and we were able to make edits as we learned more and more delegates' leanings, endorsements, and other information. Through my existing source network in PA politics, I was able to learn far more about each delegate than I ever let anyone know. Always keep the other side guessing.

As Primary Day grew closer, numerous fake lists and misinformation were pumped online, as the other side (Establishment Republicans) saw how effective our tactics were. They released lists of supposed Trump delegates, but which featured the names of one or more delegates that our intel reports had

Donald J. Trump ✅
@realDonaldTrump

"@Trumptbird: Dear I'm starting to believe that you're actually going to WIN! #Trump2016 #presidenttrump #primary pic.twitter.com/l7IcxN64gz"

REAL CLEAR POLITICS **CRUZ COLLAPSE TRUMP SURGES**

	NATL	NY	PA	MD	CT
DONALD TRUMP	45	60	48	47	50
JOHN KASICH	27	17	20	27	26
TED CRUZ	25	14	22	19	17

TRUMP ON TRACK TO PICK UP 400 MORE DELEGATES IN NEXT 2 WEEKS

4/17/16, 7:28 AM

3,826 RETWEETS **9,621** LIKES

as John Kasich or Ted Cruz supporters.

(April 17, 2016 – Trump retweeted a meme I made)

We realized there was only one way to combat the misinformation. We organized one final, official list, spent as much time as we could, making sure each of the names on it were exactly correct, and then put it in the one place we knew no one could argue with it. We asked Mr. Trump to tweet it out a few days before the election, which he gladly did.

It was amazing to see something I had helped out with tweeted out on @realDonaldTrump. We then printed thousands of the cards for our poll workers to hand out on primary day.

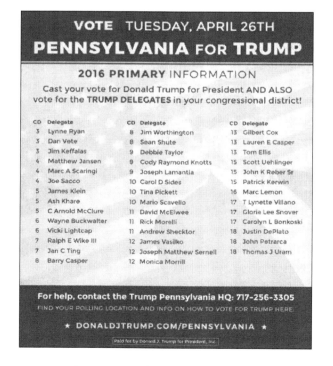

So many volunteers helped in Pennsylvania, it would be impossible to list them all, but some of the people I worked most closely with were: Tricia Cunningham, who opened a Trump office at her own expense in Pittsburgh, Leslie Rossi, who turned her entire house in to a Trump House, George Feeser, Jim Worthington, Portia Scholl, Joe Mottola, Gabe Keller, Ken Fridy, Ann Pilgreen, and Elam Stoltzfus, Kim Kay, Dan Wissert, and Lauren Casper.

On primary day itself, we identified numerous discrepancies early on with voting. People hadn't received their delegate lists, judges of elections told people to remove Trump signs from the area, people were showing up wearing MAGA hats and pins and told they couldn't vote, there were issues with voting machines in Philadelphia. These things happen each and every election day in Pennsylvania, and have ever since I first got involved in politics. Someone once told me, "Jack, no matter how much planning you do, Election Day just comes, and then it ends, and there isn't a thing you can do about it."

He was right.

The best we could do was put out what fires we could, keep the lit flowing, [what did you mean by this?] and pray that poll workers were manning their posts. As nerve-wracking as election days usually are, this one was considerably more for me. Not only because I cared so much about the candidate winning, but because I was still so far away, and extremely limited in what I could do on the ground. We did what we could to keep the war room lines of communication open with Trump supporters around the state, redeploy assets as needed, and pushed messaging in target districts as numbers came in around the state.

In the end, it all paid off. It was a massive upset. Not only did Donald John Trump win every county in Pennsylvania, he won every county of every state that voted that day in April 2016. They said "Hurricane Trump has struck the East Coast."

Trump's victory that day created a massive momentum shift that no other candidate was able to counter through the end of the primary. No one expected him to win Pennsylvania, let alone sweep it.

Winning Pennsylvania was what propelled Trump into winning the primary. His decisive win there would only foreshadow what was to come 7 months later in the Keystone State....

13 RADICAL ISLAMIC TERRORISM

One of the main issues Trump ran on was the re-branding of the War on Terror, or War on Extremism, as a war against "radical Islamic terrorism." He used this phrase on many occasions, in rallies, debates and eventually even his inaugural address. While many on the left and right have been dismissive of its use on the campaign trail, it represents a big difference between Trump and his opponents in terms of dealing with the issue of terrorism. Its use has been written about a lot in the press, but little has been said on its effectiveness. Why was it that Trump used this phrase, and why did it resonate with millions of Trump supporters?

Let's put it in context. (Pro tip: almost every single thing the media gets outraged about that Trump says or supposedly says can be understood by simply putting it in context.)

In the minds of most Americans, since at least 9/11/2001, there has been an active terror war waged against the United States. After the horrific events of that day, Americans were on a war footing. They wanted justice for what had happened. They wanted to stand up for their country. And, they wanted attacks like that day to never occur again. Safety and security were on the minds of everyone. As the wars in Afghanistan and Iraq began, many felt that "something was being done" in response to the situation. At the same time, many questions began being asked about the goals of these campaigns, especially in Iraq. Was establishing a democracy between the Tigris and Euphrates keeping Americans safer from another attack? Was it worth the thousands of killed and maimed troops and trillions of dollars spent there? As the wars slogged on, many Americans grew weary of the military actions, and wondered why so much was being done overseas but so little done at home.

Meanwhile, the adversary from 9/11 still existed. The violent strain of Islamism that spawned the Al Qaeda terror organization, the Taliban, and eventually ISIS, was at war with the West. Many would like to dispute that statement, and it has been endlessly debated in media and academic circles, but regardless of how the situation is viewed by our side, many Islamists see the conflict as a clash of civilizations between the Islamic World and the Western World. They trace the current conflict down an unbroken series of battles and campaigns back to the dawn of the Muslim era, and the first siege of Muslim forces on Constantinople in 674AD. This continued through the conquering of Jerusalem, the invasion of Spain, the sacking of Rome, the Crusades, the Ottoman Empire, and colonial powers' incursions into the Middle East and North Africa.

14 THE AMERICA FIRST RALLY AND THE RNC

After first signing on with Citizens for Trump, my first task was to get to work on the America First Rally. This started out as the only public rally supporting Donald Trump at the RNC. We had a permit from the city of Cleveland for the first day of the convention, July 2016.

From the start, it was a fight. First, the city of Cleveland put Citizens for Trump in the same area as Black Lives Matter and Antifa anarchists and rioters, which undoubtedly would have led to much violence against us, and then possibly the need for our guests or attendees to defend themselves. I've always found that its better to avoid such situations when possible. Pick your battles. From May to June 2016 in the primary season, Trump voters faced massive, horrific violence at rallies, especially in San Diego, and many threats were leveled at Cleveland pro-Trump groups, such as Citizens for Trump.

On July 7, 2016, just one week before the rally, Micah Xavier Johnson ambushed and fired upon a group of police officers in Dallas, Texas, killing five officers and injuring nine others. Johnson was reportedly angry over police shootings of black men and stated that he wanted to kill white people, especially white police officers. 2016 was a horrific year for law enforcement, with 64 officers shot dead in the line of duty. The whole situation put everyone on edge, waiting for what was going to happen next.

The security situation demanded the separation of the 2 areas. Citizens for Trump sued the City of Cleveland in federal court, even receiving support from the ACLU for our First Amendment rights. We won the case. The security perimeter around the RNC was then altered to allow our rally to be held at nearby Settler's Landing Park on the banks of the Cuyahoga River.

The rally was a HIGH Threat Alert environment with potential for rioters, infiltrators, disruptors, even assassins of our high-profile speaker. I was more worried about short knife stabbings than long-range rifles/guns used against them. Our speakers included: Alex Jones, Roger Stone, Milo Yiannopoulos, Diamond and Silk, Jan Morgan, and Joe Biggs. Not only were there multiple threats to the rally, and to our speakers, there were credible threats personally aimed at Diamond and Silk.

We enlisted great support from the Cleveland PD, Texas Rangers on horseback w/ 10 gallon hats on the line, plainclothes undercover cops from the California Highway Patrol, and we had an entire building of riot police across the street hidden, should the need arise.

We then made the decision to hire additional security for executive protection, former Delta Force operators, Seal Team VI, Army and Navy intel officers. We had an off-site realtime cyber threat fusion intel center, and onsite we had first aid, body armor and two go-cars in case of emergency. I spent the day legally armed myself with my Glock 23, 40 caliber.

The night before the rally, I stayed in a donated house outside Cleveland in which an elderly Ukrainian woman had recently passed away a few weeks before. Without AC. In the middle of July. Spared no expense. It barely had running water, most of the furniture was falling apart, the lock didn't work, it smelled like mothballs, and the front and backyards were overgrown with so many plants and trees I thought it was Jurassic Park. I slept on a bed that was little more than a cot with a cushion. I found a store nearby and stocked up on water and dry snacks like slim jims and pepperoni for the next day. I knew I'd be on my feet all day in the heat. Protein plus hydration was key.

Driving through the outskirts of Cleveland, I saw a side of the city that you might miss if you only looked at the downtown area. Shuttered homes and office buildings silently stared along the roadside. Abandoned factories loomed in the distance. Overgrown parks and playgrounds with rusted-over equipment eerily reflected good times gone by, offering a bleak perspective of the present and little hope for the future. Once-great communities that had joined to build up a great city of the American Midwest were now starving and struggling. It was something that Mr. Trump had talked about a lot on the campaign trail, but pundits had ridiculed. On the East and West Coasts, areas of the country were doing well, but in the Heartland, citizens had been getting a raw deal for years and no matter what politicians offered, nothing seemed to change. It underscored his message – Make America Great Again.

By 7am, I arrived to set up the rally. I was pretty sure I hadn't slept much the entire night. The rally was held at the bottom of a hill, with a long row of walkup houses at the top of the hill. There was a huge highway bridge above the river and above our stage, which was kept closed during the rally. We enlisted the Cleveland river police to close the river during the rally as well and they sent a patrol boat to enforce the closure.

One light rail station was at the top of the hill, with the light rail service continuing during the rally. We identified this as a threat due to anti-Trump rioters using light rails in San Diego to attack Trump voters. As they left the San Diego rally, waves of rioters swarmed out of the light rail station to attack them. The results were atrocious.

By 10am, our barriers (orange stretch netting and wooden boards) were supposed to arrive, they never did. By noon, the event began, with people streaming in unvetted and unchecked. The best we could do was keep a close eye on them. Constantly. Ohio is an open carry firearm state but we asked people to not bring long guns to our rally, handguns only. Most complied, but as always, some folks decided to cling to theirs.

As the rally began, we set up security pairs and patrol routes plus static positions at key chokepoints of the space. My own spot was escorting speakers to and from the holding area to the stage. A volunteer had arrived with a fully-converted bus with full A/C, and turned it over to us for our use. After the night I'd just had, you can imagine my relief when he let me inside for just a few minutes, totally stocked with cold bottles of water.

Just before we started the rally, I got a tap on my shoulder. I turned around, and there were 50 members of Bikers for Trump. They'd arrived with Al Baldassaro and Geraldo. Yup, Geraldo. The Bikers stood all day around the stage and provided physical security for all of our speakers. We got them water as often as we could.

JACK POSOBIEC

During the rally, I spent most of my time scanning the crowd looking for threats. They were a diverse group of people, some familiar faces, most people I'd never met from all over the country, many waving signs, and with banners and hats. Politically, I was excited at the support for Trump, but from a security perspective, each person represented a potential threat to any of our speakers. I barely remember hearing any of the speeches that day and had to watch them all later on YouTube. My day was spent looking at faces and standing between our protectees and the unknown.

We weren't sure exactly what time each speaker was arriving, because some of the speakers had extensive and fluid schedules for the week. We kept on our toes and remembered to always stay frosty. Early in the early afternoon, Roger Stone arrived via the light rail, unannounced, and shocking everyone. He gave an amazing speech.

Diamond and Silk randomly arrived in the mid-afternoon and spoke, despite the death threats to them and really roused the crowd. Milo spoke wearing a bulletproof vest covered in studs that he took off mid-speech, against all of our advice. His speech was incredibly well-received by everyone there. The Daily Show comedian Eric Andre attempted to infiltrate and crash the stage, so we let him. Alex Jones and Joe Biggs spoke, with Lee Ann McAdoo, Maggie Howell, and Millie Weaver from Infowars all attending.

Outside the bus, at one point, I met a sweaty, smiling guy wearing big red sunglasses and a beat-up green shirt. I recognized Mike Cernovich from twitter, who I'd never met in person before. "Hey, Harambe Mindset!" I called out. We shook hands and exchanged stories about what we'd been hearing going on with protestors that day.

He stayed for a while at the rally and livestreamed a lot of it on his periscope. We met up with Milo and Baked Alaska for a brief chat. Needless to say, we have all kept in touch.

On the bus at one point, Milo was sitting in the AC with a few of the Navy SEALs. They asked who he was and he said, "I'm the tech editor for Breitbart."

The SEALs nodded approvingly and said, "Nice. We love Breitbart. They tell the truth. You write anything we would know?"

Milo, looking down at his sequined bulletproof vest and golden stretch pants, replied, "Uh, well I'm not sure if my stuff is exactly what you big boys would like…but I do write about Islam."

The SEALs laughed and slapped him on the

back, "We could care less about that gay stuff, man!
You're on the right side!"

It was the same sentiment Milo would later have
at the Gays for Trump event held the next night with Jim
Hoft, Geert Wilders, and Pamela Gellar. Even though
that was the night he was banned from Twitter, everyone
around him was there to stream the speech. Trump
would protect LGBT Americans from Islamic terrorism
as much as any other American. After the Pulse
Nightclub shootings, this led to many in the community
to openly support Trump.

In the end, there were no incidents at all at the
America First Rally, the rioters stood down and did not
cross the line of the mounted police. At the end of the
day there was hardly any trash on the ground, and those
who stayed until the end helped us clean up the park. It
was a fun, positive, encouraging, and inspiring crowd.

When Trump accepted the nomination, I was
sitting squarely in the room. Roger Stone had given us a
set of tickets for all our hard work at the America First
Rally.

I expected him to give a perfunctory speech,
remarking on the nomination, and probably making
comments about the fact he was not part of the
establishment, and not having previously been in
government. Instead, Trump used the speech, with
millions of eyes on him, to deliver a blistering 77-minute
red-pilling of the world, laying bare every major issue in
the United States that had been overlooked for decades. I

couldn't believe it. No politician would ever give a speech like this. Only Trump had the platform, and the positioning to speak plainly and clearly of every crisis

plaguing America.

Deteriorating infrastructure, rampant crime in inner cities, vanishing manufacturing, a declining middle class, an unsupported military, embattled police officers and law enforcement, a country sharply divided on many lines, and radical Islamic terror attacks that seemed to never end. Donald Trump stood and said:

"Our Convention occurs at a moment of crisis for our nation. The attacks on our police, and the terrorism in our cities, threaten our very way of life. Any politician who does not grasp this danger is not fit to lead our country.

Americans watching this address tonight have seen the recent images of violence in our streets and the chaos in our communities. Many have witnessed this violence personally, some have even been its victims.

I have a message for all of you: the crime and violence that today afflicts our nation will soon come to an end. Beginning on January 20th 2017, safety will be restored.

The most basic duty of government is to defend the lives of its own citizens. Any government that fails to do so is a government unworthy to lead.

It is finally time for a straightforward assessment of the State of our Nation.

I will present the facts plainly and honestly. We cannot afford to be politically correct anymore.

So if you want to hear the corporate spin, the carefully-crafted lies, and the media myths, the Democrats are holding their convention next week.

But here, at our convention, there will be no lies. We will honor the American people with the truth, and nothing else."

15 GIVE PEACE A CHANCE, HILLARY AND THE DNC

One of the major differences between the RNC and the DNC was in the level of security, and the suppression of free speech. At the RNC, thanks to the Citizens for Trump lawsuit, the security perimeter was reduced to the area directly around the arena.

Demonstrators and protesters were able to position themselves in Cleveland so that delegates, media, and other attendees would all see them. Media Row in Cleveland was situated outside the security zone and many members of the press and Trump campaign surrogates interacted directly with the public there.

This was not the case at the DNC in Philadelphia.

Initially, I was excited that the DNC was being held in Philadelphia. Philadelphia is my hometown. It is where I grew up, where I attended college, and it is where I began my career in politics. I thought that there would be much to do and see with the convention in town, even if it was not the convention of my party. Sadly, this was not meant to be. Instead, Pennsylvania Governor Tom Wolf, a Democrat, received instructions from the Hillary Clinton campaign to put freedom of speech on lockdown. Philadelphia was turned into a fortress.

At the time of the DNC, Philadelphia was a police state.

Large metal chains and fences were erected all around the arena, and even around the parking lot for the arena. Demonstrators were fenced in by Hillary Clinton and kept out of sight from the media and the delegates.

To enter the arena complex, an attendee had to drive through the back entrance in the security wall and have a specific parking pass, or be forced to take a shuttle bus from the designated parking area into the secured zone. Hillary Clinton famously stated that she would go to Philadelphia at the convention to build bridges not walls. At the Philadelphia convention, Hillary Clinton built the largest wall that Philadelphia has ever seen.

Undeterred, many protesters and Bernie Sanders supporters took to these streets uptown by Philadelphia City Hall, far away from Hillary's coronation. Other protesters descended on FDR Park outside of the barricades. It was there that the largest protest took place, and I stood there watching events unfold firsthand: American flags were burned, a mock funeral was held for the DNC (complete with a coffin), police were harassed, and a few brave Trump supporters were assaulted.

At one point, the protesters attacked the barricades so forcefully that they pulled down the security fence. Police officers rushed into the crowd, putting their lives on the line to protect those inside without question.

While most of the people simply wanted their

voices heard, some of the protesters wanted to agitate and harass the police officers further. The protester who pulled down the barricades was arrested; his friends then attempted to start a chant of "fuck the police." Many of the demonstrators did not want to go along with this, and at that point, I asked someone if I could use their megaphone. They did not know who I was, or that I was a Trump supporter. I picked up the megaphone and began singing the only hit the song I could think of, Give Peace a Chance by John Lennon.

The crowd began to sing in unison with me and instead of rushing the barricade, I sat down and began urging others to sit down with me. This deescalated the situation, and allowed the police officers to stand their ground peacefully while the barricade was repaired.

I do not know what sort of incident would have taken place had I not started singing and encouraging the crowd to sit down, but events were going down a bad path. And in the Navy, I was trained to always take action to mitigate a bad situation before it occurs.

Weeks later, it was learned that many of the

agitators were in fact paid operatives of the Hillary
Clinton campaign engaging in a practice known as bird-
dogging. This practice was employed at many Trump
events in order to spark violence and make headlines.
Once people knew what to look for, and once the story
was exposed, these incidents begin to stop.

The Philadelphia police state was a
foreshadowing of how a Hillary Clinton America would
have looked. On TV, everything would appear to be
perfect. Perfect smiles, perfect clothing, and a perfect
audience clapping along in unison with dear leader.
Meanwhile, outside, away from cameras, protests erupt
in the streets and thousands cried out for justice—only to
be ignored, as their complaints did not fit the narrative.
Anyone who wants to see what it was like during those
dark nights in Philadelphia, can look to YouTube,
Facebook Live, or Periscope. Where you won't find them

is anywhere in the mainstream media.

16 LETS TALK ABOUT PSYOPS

Two terms used throughout 2016 were psyops and gaslighting. These psychological manipulation tactics were used in great measure by both the mainstream media, and the DC establishment in order to prevent Donald Trump from achieving victory. Understanding these tactics will allow anyone to better see through them when employed, but even in many cases, they are difficult to detect given their intrinsically subversive nature and tendency to blend fact and fiction.

Psychological operations (PSYOPs) are planned operations to convey selected information and indicators to audiences to influence their emotions, motives, and objective reasoning, and ultimately the behavior of governments, organizations, groups, and individuals.
Gaslighting or gas-lighting is a form of psychological abuse in which a victim is manipulated into doubting their own memory, perception, and sanity. Instances may range from the denial by an abuser that previous abusive incidents ever occurred up to the staging of bizarre events by the abuser with the intention of disorienting the victim.
Television is an advertising medium, by definition. Televisions have been weaponized, and never more so than in the 2016 election. Media analyst Dr. Marshall McLuhan famously said in 1964, "The medium is the message." Dr. McLuhan prophetically explained that the media itself affects society and social attitudes. For example, a story on a news channel about any particular crime has nothing to do with the actual crime. Instead, the news story has everything to do with manipulating a

change in public attitude towards the crime. It is the construction of a narrative that matters, not the actual facts of any specific story.

Army Field Manual 33-1-1 gives further objectives of PsyOps: stimulate dissension within opponents' ranks, undermine confidence in opponents' leadership and aims, lower the morale and efficiency of opponents, encourage disagreement between elements of the opposition that have grievances between each other, and interfere with opponent's communication systems. It outlines a divide-and-conquer strategy of demoralization and fracturing. When coming up against a solidified force, PsyOps are used to break up that force and create divisions among its strongest elements.

The mainstream media, to include Fox News, seemed to be operating directly out of the Army Field Manual on PsyOps throughout 2016. Polls and Electoral College maps were frequently used to demoralize Trump voters, by attempting to give the impression that Trump had no way to win the election. Mainstream media used some of the most unreliable (rigged) polls as psyops against Trump.

One of the most accurate political polls, the USC Dornsife/Los Angeles Times "Daybreak" poll (Which called both of Obama's elections correctly), consistently had Trump tied to 7% up among likely voters when asking "Who would you vote for?") throughout September and October. Other less accurate and purposely skewed polls show Hillary ahead by oversampling Democrats by 10 to 15 points amounts, even, recently, showing Hillary ahead by as much as 13% on the same day the LA Times poll had Trump up by 3%.

Oversampling simply means putting more Democrats into a poll than will likely vote in a given election. Late in October, an ABC News poll had Hillary Clinton leading Donald Trump by 12 points. Not reported in the headline was that 9% more Democrats than Republicans were sampled in the poll. Playing with polls is a common Democrat-media propaganda tactic. In an email released by Wikileaks, Democrat operative Tom Matzzie admitted the tactic, stating: "I want to get your (polling firm) people to recommend oversamples for our polling before we start in February, I want to get this all compiled into one set of recommendations so we can maximize what we get out of our media polling." Many times, mainstream media would use polling conducted by Hart Research Associates/Public Opinion Strategies, which frequently had Hillary up in double-digits over Trump. Hart Research was led by Geoff Garin who at the same time was working for Hillary's campaign, running a SuperPAC called PrioritiesUSA which dumped millions into the firm. Simply put, Hillary was paying for her own poll results, and the entire mainstream media reported on them as fact.

Many other psyops were coordinated between Hillary and the media, exposed in emails released by Wikileaks:

1. Clinton Staff hosts private "off-the-record cocktail party" with 38 "influential" reporters, journalists, editors, and anchors (from 16 different mainstream media outlets including CNN, NBC, CBS, NYT, MSNBC, & more) with the stated goal of "framing the race."

2. Donna Brazile (CNN contributor and DNC Chairman) leaked CNN town hall questions to Hillary Clinton's staff prior to the debate.

3. Clinton campaign and the New York Times coordinating attack strategy against Trump.

4. Glen Thrush, POLITICO's chief political correspondent and senior staff writer for POLITICO Magazine, sends John Podesta an article for his approval. Writes: "Please don't share or tell anyone I did this. Tell me if I f***ed up anything."

5. Huffington Post contributor Frank Islam writes to John Podesta in an email titled "My blogs in the Huffington Post," says "I am committed to make sure she is elected the next president." "Please let me know if I can be of any service to you."

6. Clinton staffer "Placing a story" with Politico / New York Times: "place a story with a friendly journalist" "we have a very good relationship with Maggie Habermann of Politico" "we should shape likely leaks in the best light for HRC."

7. John Podesta receiving drafts of New York Times articles before they were published, Clinton staff "placing a story with a friendly at the AP (Matt Lee or Bradley Klapper)."

8. Clinton staff colluding with New York Times and Wall Street Journal to paint Hillary's economic policies in a "progressive" light.

9. CNBC panelist colluding with John Podesta on

what to ask Trump when he calls in for an interview.

10. Clinton staff appearing to control the release times of Associated Press articles.

Perhaps one of the most demoralizing psyops to Trump supporters was Fox News. Fox News is controlled opposition. Controlled opposition is when a deliberate attempt is made to either create an opposing effort to any existing power base or to obtain control of any opposition to one's own efforts. In this case, Fox News parades itself as the "conservative alternative" to mainstream news, but in reality, is a facet of mainstream news itself. Its role is to bring in voters who identify as Republican and create the illusion of a free dialogue or alternative reporting, but engage on only a specific set of pre-defined safe issues. They will use hosts like Hannity and now Tucker Carlson who have big enough platforms to not be co-opted to bring in conservatives and Republicans, but then they will throw false narratives and abject lies to demoralize Trump supporters. No Fox News host was worse than Megyn Kelly, who has now been thoroughly discredited and fired from the station after viewers abandoned her transparent direct assaults on Trump and Trump supporters. It should come then, as no surprise, that Fox News parent corporation News Corp donated $3,002,926 to Bill and Hillary Clinton numerous political campaigns over the years. In addition, the News Corporation Foundation is listed on the Clinton Foundation website as a donor between $500,001 and $1,000,000, and owner Rupert Murdoch is listed as a Clinton Foundation donor $1,000,001 and $5,000,000.

Had Trump and Clinton ran in 1992, there is no question that Clinton would have won, given the absolute monopoly the mainstream media held on the dissemination of information at that time. However, in 2016, social media and the internet have democratized information, and allowed individual content creators to spread news to others throughout the world. It has also allowed independent media organizations to take rise, such as Infowars, Breitbart, Rebel Media, Drudge Report, FreeDomainRadio, The Daily Caller, and the Rubin Report. These outlets routinely challenge narratives and tropes found in mainstream media, and for their efforts are routinely derided and no-platformed by government and the Left, all in attempt to keep their massive, fine-tuned psyop running smoothly.

Don't fall for fake news.

17 HILLARY'S HEALTH

Donald Trump and Hillary Clinton are two of the oldest presidential candidates ever to run. Believe it or not, Donald Trump is the oldest person to ever be elected president. Just don't expect him to act it. Donald Trump was depicted by the media as someone in relatively good shape, a bit overweight, but still kicking at the age of 69, turning 70 on the campaign trail in June. Although a select few on the left did question Donald Trump's habit of only sleeping 3-4 hours a day. Hillary on the other hand has had a long battle with several health issues. You might call it a siege campaign. The mainstream media in 2016 made a habit of categorically disregarding any and all claims of the candidate's ailing health, trying to cast reasonable observations as both frivolous and conspiratorial. Indeed, Hillary had put out numerous official statements on her health issues for over a decade before her second failed presidential run. The key point is that the mainstream media ignored

Hillary's health issues, and it was a story that was broken entirely by grassroots media and citizen-journalists.

Hillary's first of many health problems started late in 2005, when she fainted during a 9/11 memorandum. Seriously, she did. Google it. Predictably, the mainstream media treated it as an isolated incident, but the next several years would prove otherwise. In May of 2009, Hillary emailed her aide, Huma Abedin that she wasn't feeling like taking the bus – in a message later revealed by Wikileaks. The then-Secretary of State emailed, "Do you think we could get a plane for Westchester for the flight back tonight? It's going to rain all day and I still don't feel great so the idea of playing a guessing game with the shuttle is really burdensome to me." Interesting email. Not necessarily proof of a health issue, so let's keep going down this line of inquiry.

Just a few weeks later in June 2009, Hillary Clinton fell and broke her elbow, keeping her out of work for several weeks. Her longtime henchman Sydney Blumenthal emailed her a heart-warming "Get Well" message on June 21, 2009. "Hope you are resting comfortably. Please take this as an excuse to get some much needed rest."

Two years later, video surfaced in 2011 of Hillary tripping and falling while boarding an airplane. In 2012, Hillary fell again, leaving her concussed. Her press aide reached out to NFL Commissioner Roger Goodell inquiring about advice, both with the concussion and dealing with negative press. If you haven't seen Will Smith's movie Concussion, I recommend it. Goodell's NFL organization is masterful at covering up evidence and reports of medical situations with both players and former players, and went to great lengths to keep this information away from the public. Sound familiar?

Later, in December 2012, while battling a stomach virus, Hillary fainted again. The cause was then said to be dehydration, after repeated inquiries as to what kind of stomach virus caused fainting. During the same month of December 2012, Huma Abedin spoke of Hillary in an email saying that she was, "often confused." Near the end of 2012, Hillary was admitted to a hospital, thanks in part to the discovery of a blood clot in her brain, discovered during a follow-up appointment from her concussion. At that time, Hillary was given blood thinners and advised to resign from her role at the State Department. Hillary did so in the following month, and Obama promptly replaced her with John Kerry. Even with all of that open and acknowledged in the past regarding her medical history, the mainstream media insisted that to question anything regarding her health was nothing more than a "conspiracy theory" – and painted Donald Trump personally as a misogynist for his repeated comments about Mrs. Clinton's "stamina."

Fast forward to campaign 2015, and Hillary's health was already a hot topic among most independent websites and blogs. Unsurprisingly, the mainstream media kept things hush hush, as they were poised for the anticipated Clinton vs Bush race. Several prominent doctors including Dr. Marc Siegal, Dr. David Samdi, Dr. Lee Hieb, and Dr. Jane Orie among others, voiced their concerns about Mrs. Clinton's health as a future world leader. Naturally, left-wing comedians were dispatched to mock anyone that even dared mention her majesty's health. Stephen Colbert joked that he learned he had started menopause thanks to the same research methods Hillary's health critics used, the internet.

A few weeks later, Huffington Post contributor David Seaman wrote two articles questioning Hillary's health: "Hillary Clinton's Health is Super (Aside From Seizures, Lesions and Adrenalin Pens)" and "Donald Trump Challenges Hillary Clinton To Health Records Duel." Each was a reasonable reaction to videos and evidence that have been in the public eye for years. However, that did not stop Huffington Post from promptly removing the two articles, and terminating

Seaman's affiliation with the site. Seaman then took to the internet, to inform curious viewers, that he is in fine mental health, and should he end up dead in a few days, heed the news with caution. Other books have outlined the trail of researchers and writers that have gone missing or worse, while in the investigation of House Clinton.

Online, a popular meme started by Mike

Cernovich became #HillarysStools – after noticing that

every time the former First Lady appeared on stage,

there was a stool strategically placed for her to sit while she shared the stage with other speakers. It became

something of a game for internet sleuths to find images of #HillarysStools in pictures from throughout the campaign, and even further back into her career. Other photos were found of her leaning on railings, being helped up flights of stairs by her staff, and even one speech where she was propped up by Secret Service. The commenters all realized that something was going on with Hillary's health that for some inexplicable reason, was not discussed in the mainstream press, cable news, or political establishment. By 2016, the court of political discourse had already been democratized by the internet, but no one had told the media gatekeepers yet.

(Hillary Clinton and her many public stools)

September 2016 saw another 9/11 health event

for Mrs. Clinton. On a sunny Sunday morning during the

15th anniversary of America's most infamous day, Hillary Clinton spoke to several families of the fallen at the memorial in New York City. She was only there for an hour and thirty minutes, but left abruptly; her staff announcing it was due to heat exhaustion. It was 79 degrees that morning. As she left, her staff prevented any reporters from following her as she made her way to her van. However, her staff had forgotten it was the Current Year. While the entirety of the mainstream media turned off their cameras, or turned them away from Hillary Clinton, a lone man on the side of the road turned his iPhone towards her. The man was Zdenek Gazda, a Czeck immigrant and firefighter in New Jersey. That day, his twitter account @zdazda66 had about 2,000

followers. Mr. Gazda saw Hillary and her entourage walking strangely past him, and had the mindfulness to pull out his iPhone and begin recording video. He posted it immediately, and the rest is history. The video showed Mrs. Clinton, a candidate for Leader of the Free World, collapsing into the arms of her security and Secret Service.

The security teams looked like they had prepared for this, as they immediately reacted with a pre-planned response drill, supporting her under her arms and carrying her to a waiting black van. That day, writer Scott Adams declared "The race for president is probably over." He continued: "When it comes to American psychology, there is no more powerful symbol of terrorism and fear than 9/11. When a would-be Commander-in-Chief withers – literally – in front of our most emotional reminder of an attack on the homeland, we feel unsafe. And safety is our first priority. Hillary Clinton just became unelectable."

That video was the tweet heard round the world. Mr. Gazda's short clip was viewed over 10 million times, and played non-stop on cable news. There was no way to put it back in the bottle. After months of smears and clamoring about conspiracy theories, the entire mainstream media and breathlessly shrill Democrat Party operatives were silenced. That day, with one simple video, a break in the simulation appeared. The media unequivocally lost their narrative monopoly in 2016, and will never gain it back. The combination of social media and smartphones has led to a revolution in information-sharing and the ability of one person to capture a story, and have it beamed to eyes, ears, and minds collectively across the globe. Reality itself had shifted, as our awareness of it and perception had widened to an immeasurable scope. On September 11, 2016, one man really did change the world.

Thanks, Zdenek.

18 THE FAKE NEWS MEDIA

As mentioned before, the credibility of the Main Stream Media utterly unraveled during the 2016 campaign season… and it was a glory to behold. Most avid followers of politics knew that most, if not all, mainstream media outlets were agenda and narrative driven, instead of fact and truth driven. Sometimes this was due to advertising dollars, and sometimes due to ownership bias. Still, long-established brands like The New York Times, Washington Post, and CNN were seen by the public as presenting facts from an unbiased perspective.

Here are just a few examples of how the general public has been sorely misled over the past few years:

> • 2000: CBS News reported on 1 million disenfranchised black voters in the 2000 Presidential election. The report claimed that

dogs and hoses were used to turn would-be black voters away. How much evidence was given to support this claim? Zero. Even so, the U.S. Commission on Civil Rights conducted a full-scale, 6 month investigation. Not a single shred of wrongdoing was found, and the case was dismissed. Even with these facts, the left loves this myth, and they never stop talking about it.

• 2004: CBS's Dan Rather reported on forged memos that depicted George W. Bush refusing military orders. This aired 2 months before the 2004 election, and were promptly found to be false. Rather resigned in disgrace (if only news anchors still had some smidgen of shame left).

• 2009: In September of 2009, less than a year after Obama had been inaugurated, Tea Partiers rallied 1 million plus protestors to march against increased federal spending, and more specifically, ObamaCare. ABC and mainstream sources reported that only 60,000 protestors were out in force. In the early days of social media, pictures and video abounded on Facebook proving the media reports wrong (foreshadowing the Trump and Clinton crowd attendance reporting in 2016).

• 2014: In Ferguson, Missouri during the Summer of 2014, Police Officer Darren Wilson shot Michael Brown. CNN, NBC, FoxNews, MSNBC and pretty much every single other major news outlet reported that Michael Brown had his hands up and was shot several times in the back. For days, the newsmedia repeated the meme of "Hands Up Don't Shoot," even with a panel of CNN commentators holding their hands up while the title ran on the screen below with the phrase. Riots ensued in Ferguson, with many businesses destroyed and looted. This phrase came by way of an anecdote from a single source. Following the medical report on Michael Brown, as well as numerous eyewitness reports, this was completely disproven.

• 2016. The Washington Post and Miami Herald claimed, yet again, "The AR-15 Myth." ISIS terrorist Omar Mateen attacked partygoers at Pulse Night Club in Orlando, Florida, killing 49 and wounding 52. Both the Post and the Herald said the weapon used was an AR-15. They had no evidence to support that claim, but have singled out the rifle in so many other reports that it has become something of a go-to for the media (along with calling every handgun a Glock). The actual gun was a Sig Sauer MCX.

• 2016. Perhaps the biggest media fail was the most recent. Almost every single mainstream media outlet had Hillary Clinton winning the presidential election in an effortless landslide. NY Times and its fabled pollster Nate Silver even went as far to say that Mrs. Clinton had a 98% chance of winning on the day of the election.

It is human nature to have biases, no matter how hard anyone tries to work against them. From now on, people expect their news to come with a bias, and in many ways, welcome it. Unlike the "liberal" news outlets that hide behind the masquerade of an "unbiased, facts only" persona. Consumers of news products need to move forward, and hold news outlet giants accountable. No more fake news.

Here, in no particular order, is a list of Fake News created by mainstream media in 2016. (Note, this list is far from comprehensive. I will leave space for you to add in your favorites)

- Trump mocked a reporter with a disability (False)
- Trump criticized the wife of Khizr Khan (False)
- Trump called for the assassination of Hillary Clinton (False)
- Trump admitted on tape to sexual assault (False)
- Trump claimed Mexicans can't be judges (False)
- Trump said all Mexicans are rapists (False)
- Trump refused to disavow David Duke (False)
- Trump was sued for child sexual abuse (Very False)
- Trump was tied to the mafia (False)
- Trump University was a scam (False)
- Trump's businesses all ended in bankruptcy (False)
- Trump was accused of marital rape (False)
- Trump's campaign manager assaulted Michelle Fields (False)
- Trump broke the law to do business in Cuba (False)
- Trump is a racist (Zero evidence)
- Trump kicked a baby out of his rally (False)
- Trump will drop out of the race, secretly supports Hillary, doesn't want to win (NOPE!)

19 PEPE THE FROG

It's not a secret that Hillary Clinton stinks when it comes to pandering to Millennial voters. I sympathize with her in the fact that it must be hard to get anybody to like you when you are a walking, breathing, she-devil. Hillary tried the "Pokemon Go to the polls" tactic once Pokemon Go came out, and she was justifiably met with jeers and a bunch of shaking heads. Among the Democrats, Bernie was the obvious choice for young people. While both were old enough to be a grandparent, Bernie spoke clearly, he didn't pontificate and poeticize his words as Hillary liked to do. Granted, Trump is old enough to be a grandparent to most millennials, so how did he resonate with them? Pepe the Frog.

Pepe the frog first originated from a comic series written by Matt Furie. The comic series was called "Boy's Club." Pepe was first introduced into Popular culture in 2008, when he started making the rounds on MYspace, Gaia Online, and 4chan. By 2015 Pepe had become one of the most prolific figures in 4chan and some of the other more modern social medias such as Twitter and Facebook. Katy Perry has tweeted a picture, same for Nicki Minaj, and Wendys even temporarily included Pepe as a mascot. Donald Trump couldn't resist the trend.

In October of 2015, he retweeted a video of the
Pepe meme, The video repeatedly uttered the
phrase "You can't stop the Trump." This is
where Hillary should have learned a few lessons
from Trump. Trump did not go above and
beyond to try and be relatable with Millenials,
because he knows if they respect anything, it's
being genuine. Trump knows how cringe-worthy
it is when Dads and older gentlemen try too hard
to remain hip, so he doesn't make a conscious
effort to try. Trump found the perfect medium
for acknowledging the humor young people
have, but still steering away from trying to be a
part of it.

However, in the beginning of 2016,
Pepe took on a new, becoming the "face" of the
Alt-Right. While the "Alt-Right" has several
definitions, I have personally always considered
it to mean someone who is on the right, but not a
traditional Republican. Several within the Alt-
Right have used the meme, no doubt about that,
but some claim that it is a misattribution to place
Pepe solely with the Alt-Right. Still, The Anti-
Defamation League added Pepe the Frog to their
ever increasing database of hate symbols. This
led Pepe's creator, Matt Furie, to publicly voice
his dismay in the public's use of Pepe as a form
of hate mongering. Matt was far from correct.

Then Pepe's true form was revealed – Kek.

Kek is the deification of the primordial concept of
darkness in ancient Egyptian religion. Like all four

dualistic concepts in the Ogdoad, Kek's male form was depicted as a frog, or as a frog-headed man, and the female form as a snake, or a snake-headed woman. As a symbol of darkness, Kek also represented obscurity and the unknown, and thus chaos. Also, Kek was seen as that which occurred before light, thus was known as the bringer-in of light.

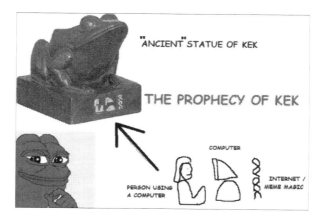

A Brief History of Kekistan

(From kekistan.wikia.com)

"The Kekistanis or Kekistani People are a diverse ethno-linguistic group primarily comprised of the speakers of the Kekish languages. Kekistanis are proud people with over 2,000 years of history. Unfortunately, much of the history of the Kekistanis has been either lost or destroyed during the Great Exodus after the SJWs' expulsion of the Kekistani people from their homeland. However their culture is being reborn during the ongoing Great Meme War. In addition to the war, SJWs and normies have consistently been disrespecting and denouncing Kekistani culture, which must be stopped.

In the beginning of their civilization, the first Kekistani people settled in the very fertile valleys and coasts of what is now Iran and began to master the arts of farming memes and shitposting. Kekistani memes were in high demand across the bronze-age civilizations for their superior quality and quantity and as such the Kekistani people became rich and the fractured kingdoms of the Kekistani prospered.

This was the Golden age of Kekistan, which lasted from 2000 BC to around 200 BC. Then, in around 200 BC, the jealousy of the wealth of the Kekistanis led to the combined invasion of Kekistani lands by the Empire of Normies and the Social Justice Matriarchy, which led to the downfall of the kingdoms of Kekistan. this also staged the beginning of the deportation and genocide of hundreds of thousands of Kekistani peoples. The last Kekistani kingdom fell in ~2 BC.

Kekistan Genocide
Archeologists believe the fall of the final kingdom led to what is known as The Great Exodus, with the last of the Kekistani armies holding back the hordes of the Normies and SJWs while the citizens fled across Mesopotamia. The sacrifices of the Kekistani armies would become the stuff of legends in the annals of Kekistani history. The Kekistani people then settled in Egypt and started to re-master their crafts, as much of their knowledge was lost during the war. Back in the homeland, SJWs and Normies had enslaved the Kekistani people, attempting to force them to make memes for the use of the SJWs and Normies, however the Kekistani people refused which led to the Kekistani Genocide, where the culture and history of the Kekistani people was nearly wiped out and the Kekistani people being slaughtered in their homeland. By 20 AD there was less than 100 Kekistani people left in traditional Kekistani lands.

The Kekistani people toiled in Egypt, life being hard and full of fear of the SJWs and Normies.

but the Kekistanis were able to survive because of Chapter 5 in the Book of Kek that talked about the rise of the peoples of Kek, so the Kekistanis waited for centuries for the destined day. It is rumored that some Kekistani people joined the First Crusade in retaking Jerusalem, but no evidence has been found.

By 2016 the Kekistani people had spread across nearly the entire world with small minorities in many western countries. However, a great menace to the Kekistani people arrived in the form of Hillary the Crooked, who sought to destroy and slander the Kekistani people and the Prophet Pepe. All seemed lost for the Kekistani people until the destined savior arrived. God Emperor Donald J. Trump, ordained by Kek, accepted the mantle of Kek to fight Hillary the Crooked and the forces of the SJWs, who had grown far too powerful. The Kekistani people rejoiced and flocked to their savior, sparking the Great Meme War which is still ongoing. The Great Meme War was in a stalemate for most of 2016 until in November when the Kekistani people won a great victory in securing God Emperor Trump the presidency of the United States."

20 SOCIAL MEDIA CHANGING POLITICS

Since before America was even a country, citizens got their information through print. Whether it be newspapers or journals, people would get their information in a paper form, sometimes taking weeks to get to them. It was this way until the early 1900's, when the television was invented. After the television was refined to include live broadcasts, Americans and the rest of the world were now able to receive up to the minute information regarding their politics, sports, and other informational or entertainment needs. During much of the second half of the 20th century, Americans got their news and civics information primarily through a few dominant sources, usually a local newspaper that had a relative monopoly on local information, or one of three major television networks.

While television helped bring immediacy to news distribution, it was still susceptible to corruption. As I mentioned above, three networks dominated the market, which meant the news came with a bit of censorship. The news stations became more and more political and agenda-based while still claiming to be "unbiased" In more recent times this has become blindingly obvious. The rise of social media in the 21st century helped give information back to the American people, as the people were now less reliant on those gargantuan cable networks.

For one, Facebook and other sites like Twitter give users the feel of a "casual acquaintance." Meaning that you may not be buddy buddy with your online, "friend" but you acknowledge his presence. Experts are still sure that an acquaintance that has a stronger tie to friend will be influential, especially when it comes to political affiliation, but it is still unclear how much these internet acquaintances can affect voter outcome. It's no secret Trump played Twitter like a fiddle. He started doing this primarily during Obama's second term, never fearing to take to the social media platform to throw in a few insults. Trump's use and abuse of Twitter was paramount to his successful grassroots campaign. Many of Trump fans coalesced around the Trump/America First movement by first finding and supporting each other online, then meeting in the real world to organize and voice their support. This is very similar to the phenomena known as the "Silent Majority". This is where Trump supporters were not confident enough to voice their opinions in their workplace, school, or community so naturally, they took to social media platforms. This explains why the polling was so misleading. Maybe these members of the silent majority were not being truthful with who they intended to vote for, or maybe major news networks are not objective anymore.

21: AMERICAN NATIONALISM

It's no secret that Americans have always been considered a patriotic country, I would make the argument that our citizens are among the most patriotic in the world. However, slowly, Americans were losing that comraderie that brought us together. Leftists pushed their immigrant agenda, open borders, massive wide-scale refugee acceptance, and identity politics practices. It's a shame our left could not learn lessons from the European crises. Massive waves of immigration have flipped the European Union upside down. Crime is up, rape is up, and many European cities are now showing resemblances to some third world countries. This is what happens when you drop hundreds of thousands of immigrants into a country where they have no intention of assimilating to the culture of wherever they are presiding. That, along with the threat of a Trojan horse, where members of Islamic terrorist regimens hide behind the persona of a refugee while plotting to set in motion a terrorist attack. And it happened more than

once: the France bus attack, England train, Brussels airport; the list goes on. This is probably the main reason Brexit happened. The UK wanted to take back their state sovereignty, much like Trump and the majority of Americans.

Trump promised to curb the illegal immigration that has plagued our country for too many years. Many Americans were glad to hear this. More than 10 million immigrants preside in our great country, some of them criminals, most of them just looking for a better life. Still, rules are there for a reason, and our country is one of the greatest countries in the world. It's no secret hat most of the world would give a few fingers for a shot at the American Dream. Which is why millions of wanna-be immigrants wait in a metaphorical line, hoping for citizenship. Why can't the left empathize with them, as illegals cut them in line, bypassing law and order? Not only did these illegals take an opportunity not meant for them, but when they got to America, they didn't appreciate the country that still gives them a great opportunity even when it's not deserved. DACA (Deferred Action for Childhood Arrivals) allows illegal immigrants to work, several private universities give illegal immigrant scholarships, and anchor baby citizenship. After all, Americans have a heart for some of these illegal immigrants that have a troubled past and truly are looking for a better future for themselves and their future generations. So it's maddening to myself personally and numerous other Americans, when some of these immigrants parade around within our countries borders, waving Mexican flags, and spouting chants

such as, "Make America Mexico". The real wonder is
why America didn't cry for Nationalism much sooner.
Trump spoke vehemently against the ever increasing
anti-American rhetoric. While the left was making cries
for open borders, Trump wanted to give better
opportunities for American born citizens. this is why he
ended up getting around 30% of the Hispanic vote, and it
should have been much more had the mainstream media
not continuously broadcasted lies about Trump's plan to
deport any non-white citizens.

America's nationalism when it comes to Muslim
refugees is a bit more tricky. America's responsibility to
the United Nations requires us to take in some of the
world's refugees, but we have the freedom to vet
whoever, however. The left claims that vetting is a
humanitarian crime, but if they look at some of the PEW
Research surveys, the left should acknowledge just how
illiberal the "peaceful" religion of Islam really is. In the
middle east, only 33% of Muslims believe that women
should have the right to request a divorce. In the
Palestinian territory, 49% of Muslims say that suicide
CAN sometimes be justified. In countries like
Afghanistan, Iraq, and the Palestinian countries, between
89 and 99% of Muslims believe that Sharia law should
be the official law of the land. The same law that
justifies the execution of women that have premarital
sex, the beheading of gays, and a regressive agenda that
goes against everything the progressive agenda fights
for. It's paradoxical for the left to want that kind of
thinking into our free country. These are some of the
factors that led to the the American people's increasing

nationalistic view. It's a tribalistic instinct to band together, and increasing scrutiny will increase that instinct.

22: POPULISM IN AMERICA

AMERICAN REVOLUTION

Many historians would actually consider the American Revolution to be a "Populist" Revolution. If you think about it, that time period closely resembles the American political movement of now. Taking back individual state sovereignty. The 13 original colonies decided no longer to live under the British monarchy, no longer subjecting to their aristocracy and authority. The initial spark began in 1765, when members of the American colonial society were growing increasingly restless with British rule. In 1765, the Sons of Liberty were founded. They capitalized on public demonstrations, boycotts, violence, and threats of violence to undermine British tax laws and make them much more difficult to enfore. In Boston, the Sons of Liberty burned the records of the vice admiralty court and looted the home of chief justice Thomas Hutchinson, fighting increasing taxes and the lack of colonial representation within the Government. The societal discontent continued to grow over the next several years, eventually surmounting in the Boston Tea Party in 1773.

GREENBACK PARTY

In 1867, the Greenback party was formed, initially led by Oliver Kelly. The mission of this party was to address the social isolation many farmers were facing across America. Much like the Freemasons and other secret societies, The Greenback party had local chapters with numerous secret passwords and rituals. Members were strictly referred to as "Grangers." The Grangers were adept at mixing work and play; they would often hold dances and other social gatherings to escape the burdens of the everyday life. It was during these events, that the Grangers would discuss how to better their situations. Many of the Grangers began to see the same problem in each of their lives. The railroad was becoming a nuisance. The Grangers lobbied for state legislatures, demanding that the train industry be regulated. Much to their efforts, several states passed "Granger" laws that would establish maximum shipping rates and efficiency. The Greenback party was a small stepping stone towards American Populism.

The Farmers Alliance, founded in 1889, took the work of the Greenbacks one step farther. The Northern and Southern Farmer's Alliances fought for many of the same issues as the Grangers, but they did what the Grangers were too passive to do: they ran for office. Several members of these alliances won seats in state legislative positions, mostly across the Great Plains. Nevertheless, farmers had a larger political voice than ever before. So what exactly did farmers want? They all faced roughly the same problem: debt. The farmers blamed the nation's monetary system. Since 1873, Congress had been enforcing that all federal money be backed up by gold. This severely limited the country's money supply, vastly benefiting the wealthy. The farmer's wanted to create inflation. Their logic was if they got $1 for each crop, with inflation they could get

$2 or even $3 per crop, thus prompting them to have to sell less product to dissolve their debt problem. This led Congress to print money that was NOT backed up by gold. This actually began happening before the Civil War, causing an inflationary effect during the war, leading to the mandate later.

POPULIST PARTY

From the graves of the Greenback party and the Farmer's alliance came the Populist Party. Populists were the first to demand a class-based taxation system, in which individuals and families that earned more money had to pay a higher percentage in taxes. This is directly similar to the system we have in place today. The Populists also fought for political reforms. In their day, United States Senators were still not purely democratically elected. Instead, they were chosen by state legislatures, which had been proven to have shades of corruption within the system. Populists demanded a constitutional amendment that would allow for the direct election of Senators by the American people. They also demanded the "Initative" a legislative action that would allow citizens, not state representatives, to vote on a bill. They thought this would make sense because most state legislators were wealthier and therefore less likely to experience the majority of issues that common folk would face during these days. They also called for the secret ballot, and a forced one-term limit for the president. Both of these ideas had little success in getting passed.

BULL MOOSE GOVERNMENT

The Bull Moose party were adamant in their belief that the government is not working for the people's best interest. Their views were very similar to the Orwellian ideas presented in both 1984 and Animal Farm. Those views included destroying the omnipresent government, and if that wasn't possible, making it as small as could be, for a start. The Bull Moose party simply believed that Government and large corporations were so intertwined, corruption was inevitable, as corporations would lobby for the politicians they wanted and the politicians would not crack down on the corporations that lobbied for them. Among other ideas, the Bull Moose party called for these:

- Strict limits and disclosure requirements on political campaign contributions

- Registration of lobbyists

- Recording and publication of Congressional committee proceedings

- Women's suffrage

- Direct election of Senators

- Primary elections for state and federal nominations

- The platform also urged states to adopt measures for "direct democracy", including:

- The recall election (citizens may remove an elected official before the end of his term)

- The referendum (citizens may decide on a law by popular vote)

- The initiative (citizens may propose a law by petition and enact it by popular vote)

- Judicial recall (when a court declares a law unconstitutional, the citizens may override that ruling by popular vote).

- New Nationalism

- Strong Defense

NOTABLE INDEPENDENT CANDIDATES

Huey Long is the most Trumpian of any on this list. He was an ardent fighter for everything he believed in, and that would permeate into his speaking. From the very beginning of his political career, Long would be labelled a demagogue from supporters of both parties, some even feared he might turn dictator should he eventually win the presidency. Huey Long won the Louisiana governor race in 1928, becoming Louisiana's 40th governor. Long would serve as governor from 1928 to 1932, where he would then hold a seat in the United States Senate. During Long's leadership as governor, many state funded systems were expanded. Systems such as schools and hospitals, primarily a system of charity hospitals that were specifically designed to help the poor. Long also sought construction of massive highways and free bridges. He did this to bring an end to rural isolation. Huey Long supported Franklin D

Roosevelt's bid for the presidency in 1932, but his support ceased in June of 1933, when Long began to plan to run against FDR in the 1936 election. One month after Long formally announced he would run for presidency, Dr. Carl Weiss shot and killed him on Capitol Hill, September 8, 1935. Dr. Weiss was Judge Benjamin Henry Pavy's son in law. Dr. Weiss shot Huey Long at 9:20pm, just minutes after "House Bill Number One" was passed, effectively removing Dr. Weiss's father in law from the bench. Huey Long ran a very similar campaign to Donald Trump, although their approach was vastly differnet in terms of redistribution of wealth. They both spoke directly to the same audience, the American working class.

ROSS PEROT

As a boy, Ross Perot grew up in Boy Scout programs. He eventually achieved the rank of Eagle Scout just around the same time he graduated from Texas High School. Perot would then go on to join the Navy, where he would have a relatively quiet tenure. In 1956, while Perot was still in the Navy, he married Margot Birmingham. Perot would leave the Navy one year later and then go on to work for IBM. Perot's tenure at IBM would only be for 5 years, but he was immediately recognized as one of the most efficient employees. Perot was so efficient that one year it only took him two weeks to fulfill his annual sales quota. Perot would always pitch ideas as to how to improve the company to his superiors, but time and time again he was ignored. As Perot continued to get frustrated with this, his time to leave had come. Perot parted with IBM in 1962, then immediately went to start a company of his own, "Electronic Data Systems." (EDS). Success was slow at first. Perot's services were declined 77 times before he landed his first contract, but once the first came, the rest followed in packs. EDS's bulk of work would come from government contracts, such as computerizing Medicare records. 6 years after EDS was founded, the stock went public and within days the stock price went from $16 to $160 a share. In 1982, 20 years after Perot started his company, he sold out to General Motors for a whopping 2.4 billion dollars.

On February 20th, 1992, Ross Perot made an appearance on Larry King Live. It was there where Perot dropped his bombshell: he would be running for president. Perot stated that he would run as an independent and urged his supporters to get his name on the ballot in every state. Perot's popularity blossomed the most after the failing candidacies of Republican Pat Buchanan and Democrat Jerry Brown. Perot campaigned with promises to balance the federal budget, oppose gun control, and rethink the Constitution. Perot's "Populism" led him to receive 18% of the Popular vote, the highest amount by a 3rd party candidate since 1912. Most of Perot's popularity is accredited to a growing discontent with the increasing partisan politics of both the Democrats and Republicans.

Even though Perot lost, he remained politically active throughout Bill Clinton's presidency, predominantly speaking out against the ever-increasing national debt. Perot ran with the Reform party in 1996, but this time he only received 8% of the vote. That would mark the end of Perot's attempts to obtain any governmental office. While his attempts at the presidency may have failed, Perot helped give a voice to American populism and politicians that may differ from the 2 major political parties. And as of 2015 he was the 129th richest man in the world.

TEA PARTY MOVEMENT

The Tea Party movement first saw light in 2009, early in Obama's inauguration. The movement was dead set against Obama's plan to bail out bankrupt homeowners. Some within the movement even went as far as to call him a Socialist. (Maybe they weren't all crazy kooks after all) The Tea Party group fought for simple, conservative principles such as balancing the federal deficit, decreasing federal spending and decreasing taxes for all American people. You could say the movement is a mixture of libertarian, populist and conservative activism. A little more than 10% of Americans claim to fit the mold of this party. If you haven't been able to tell yet, the group's name derives from the famous tea party incident that occurred in 1773, when American colonials grew restless with excess British taxation, prompting them to litter the Boston Harbor with the British's tea.

Trump knew he would need the support of the Tea Party to win the presidency. In August of 2015, he told a Tea Party gathering that, "The tea party people are incredible people. These are people who work hard and love the country and they get beat up all the time by the media". In an early 2016 CNN poll, Trump narrowly edged out Ted Cruz with support among Tea Partiers with 37% of the group's support compared to Cruz's 34%. While the Tea Partiers were essentially split with their support during the primaries, National Tea Party movement co-founder and leader, Michael Johns immediately endorsed Trump as soon as he announced his plans to run for presidency in June 2015. Johns would eventually help sway the divided Tea Party towards Trump, exalting Trump as a true outsider, an outsider more likely to give non partisan Americans a voice. The Tea Party was paramount to Mr. Trump s success. Without the support of those passionate conservative members, Hillary Rodham Clinton very well could have been the 45th president of The United States.

23: THE FAILED GOP COUP

The weasel is out of the bag and his name is Paul Ryan. When the Access Hollywood tapes event happened, I was the one to break the real news around a power play made by Rep Paul Ryan, that has shamed the entire state of Wisconsin.

As it turns out, the video of Trump and Billy Bush that was leaked from unknown sources has been traced back to Ryan. The anti-Trump operatives never bothered to investigate the source. Those on the networks, the GOP establishment and the Clinton campaign were just happy it had appeared and were delighting in the feeding frenzy intent on driving him out of the race.

Ryan's little event in Wisconsin was to be the stage for him to feign his indignation and then dismiss Mr. Trump in unison with fellow operatives such as

Senator Mike Lee of Utah. When critical mass was reached, they would use an unwitting and uninvolved Governor Mike Pence as the vehicle into which to attach themselves in Trump's place.

Trump would be forced out, Pence would move to the top of the ticket and Paul Ryan would slide in. Clinton would still likely win, which is completely acceptable and the lesser of the two evils for the establishment in the GOP. They would then focus their efforts on picking up the globalist pieces with a Ryan/Rubio ticket for 2020.

Once again, those who targeted Mr. Trump underestimated him. They thought they could force him to quit, which he does not do. They also thought that Paul Ryan was equal in stature as a candidate to the man we all were demanding to be our next president.

This was a failed coup in no exaggeration of the terms. Now the participants are becoming fully exposed. There will be a price for them to pay.

Here is an account of my reporting from the DC site Political Storm:

WASHINGTON–(Political Storm) On the surface, most people, when they think of what happened with Donald Trump's Access Hollywood interview right before the second debate, would think that Hillary's campaign put it out there for the purposes of destroying Trump in the second debate.

There might actually be more to it. Meet Jack Posobiec, the Washington-based special projects director at Citizens for Trump, who was at Trump Tower in New York City, having meetings with the campaign during that politically-turbulent weekend. Posobiec posited, in an interview with Your Voice Radio on October 11, that it was actually GOP establishment figures–namely Paul Ryan — that were plotting a coup against the Republican nominee.

Posobiec claims may be backed up by a Howie Kurtz Fox News Mediabuzz interview, before the debate, of David Farenthold, the author who had trouble saying whether his source wanted to destroy Trump's candidacy.

As Posobiec tells it,"what we saw from the inside and what I'm hearing now, piecing together what was going on was that this was actually an attempted coup of the GOP establishment reasserting themselves over the party that they really feel that they had lost and in some ways were very correct on that."

Posobiec went on to say, "They were basically going around telling people that Donald Trump was going to drop out of the race and that if you want to un-endorse Trump you better do it now so when he drops out you won't look like you ever stopped endorsing him and the Democrats can't hit you."

GOP elected officials were told by leadership sources that Trump was going to be leaving the race. "All these people thought that Trump was going to drop out of the race, all these elected officials, so beforehand trying to look like they have the inside scoop, they all start endorsing him. Then they were told: here's how it is going to work- Trump's going to drop out of the race [Trump's vice presidential nominee, Indiana Governor Mike] Pence will move up to the top of the ticket. Now Pence was not involved in any of this, and they knew that Hillary was going to win. Quote unquote knew. The plan was Ryan-Rubio 2020," added Posobiec.

The attempted coup plan that could have doomed Mr. Trump's candidacy, according to Trump campaign activists, would have occurred the Saturday before the debate at Paul Ryan's Wisconsin GOP Fall Fest in Elkhorn, Wisconsin. Trump was expected to attend but was uninvited at the last moment due to the leaked Access Hollywood tape.

"So the idea was they were trying to orchestrate it so that Trump would drop out, Pence goes to the event and Ryan becomes the kingmaker because Pence goes to the Ryan event and becomes the nominee there. Right, see how that was supposed to play out?" Posobiec said.

Pence was supposed to attend the event, despite Trump being uninvited, but the campaign changed its plans."I think Pence really did intend to go at one point to represent Mr. Trump. I believe Trump asked him not to attend the event because it was learned that the tape was initially leaked by a Paul Ryan staffer." added Posebiec.

Posobiec was so skeptical of the media coverage that Pence might ever consider dropping out that he checked the flight logs of Pence's plane.

"He never once changed his flight plan. He never changed his flight plan from what he was going originally to do, a fundraiser for Mr. Trump in Providence, RI. He attended that fundraiser, he spoke very highly of Mr. Trump there, he had a rally the day after debate. After the debate on Monday, he again spoke highly of Mr. Trump. So, the GOP that were sort of the establishment, that was pushing all of this stuff, had a ton of egg on their face right now. Their lies had been exposed for all to see. Mr. Trump was never going to drop out or Mr. Pence or any number of false narratives thrown around all weekend" added the special projects director for Citizens for Trump.

Media coverage of the event according to the YourVoice radio interviewer Cari Kelemen was skewed as to who was distancing themselves from whom.

"It looked for a minute over the weekend, if you were kind of paying attention, that Pence was distancing himself from Trump, but what really happened was Pence was distancing himself from Ryan".

Trump campaign activists do however, describe a frantic effort on Saturday to keep the campaign from disappearing into thin air.

"But Trump and his people and some us on the inside who are true believers, as we kind of call ourselves, got the information to the right people about what is going and said - don't go to that event, just do what you were going to do. Nobody is dropping out. None of the voters actually care about this thing. This all in everybody's heads, all that the media is pushing" Posobiec said.

The fury on social media was just as intense against the GOP establishment effort to doom Trump's bid. "I was so pleasantly surprised how Trump supporters on Twitter rallied behind him on Saturday. It went from kind of quiet, to absorption and then I think the GOP leadership was hoping we would be angry at Trump. Instead, by midday on Saturday, people started getting angry for Trump. They were furious at their own party" Kelemen added.

At Trump Tower on Sunday, Posobiec observed also that the media's narrative of Trump having no support was false, as well.

"So, I am talking to the waiter at Trump Grill. Were you here yesterday when you had the big rally outside and Trump went out? He said yeah. He said "all the sudden everyone in the restaurant ran out" and he said 'Excuse me, you guys didn't pay. What are you doing?' They told him 'It's Trump! He's here!' And everyone in the entire tower ran out to be with Mr. Trump and to show their support. To rally to him at the moment. When everyone was trying to make it seem like he had no support."

Posobiec concluded his interview on YourVoice radio with a warning for Trump supporters "I would let them know unfortunately this is probably not going to be the last step. There's still a lot of time between now and

Election Day and there will be continual attempts to subvert and possibly - sabotage is a word you could use - Mr. Trump's efforts by the Paul Ryan wing of the GOP."

24: TRUMP VS HILLARY DEBATES

Entering the first debate, Hillary Clinton had a marginal lead over Donald Trump, 46% to his 41%, only a 5% difference. The first debate was held on September 26th at Hofstra University. The debate format included six fifteen-minute segments where a different topic would be introduced in each segment and each candidate would get equal speaking time. The segment topics were job creation, trade, racial relations, policing, the war on terror, job creation, and each candidate's business or political experience. Trump ended up speaking 4 minutes more than Hillary. Although Trump going over his time was not a big issue, most of the blame for that could be placed on the moderator, Lester Holt. After the debate, a entire flood of criticism came at Lester Holt, and rightfully so. Holt struggled with his authority, he couldn't keep both candidates to stick to the topics, and he failed repeatedly when trying to keep both Clinton and Trump within the speaking time limits. Holt came off as passive aggressive, wishy washy, and non confrontational. Simply put, he did not pester either candidate with hard questions, and that is what Americans wanted to see the most, specifically questions regarding Hillary Clinton's emails.

Nevertheless, the debate broke the cable television record for most viewers ever, with 84 million. And that does not even count YouTube or Facebook live streams, which some say both of those combined could have been upwards of 11 million. Although Trump clearly did not perform his best during the first debate, every poll had him losing in a landside. Dishonest media perhaps? The only poll I shall show is from the "nonbiased" Politico. This poll only asked members of the swing states, and they polled Clinton winning at 79%. I wonder why the votes didn't sway that way.

The 2nd debate was set up in the infamous

TownHall fashion, with Anderson Cooper and Martha

Raddatz sitting in as moderators. If you are unaware of

what a Townhall debate is, the audience is composed of

undecided voters, where they, along with the
moderators, would ask questions to both candidates. The
questions were set up so that half of the questions would
come from the attendants and the other half would come
from the moderators or social media. The biggest story
of this debate was the "Trumptapes". Two days before
this debate, some tapes leaked of Trump speaking in an
autobus about how he likes his women. A totally private
conversation between two men in 2005, yet it's relevant
to the 2016 presidential election. The first 15-20 minutes
of the debate was devoted entirely to this topic of
grabbing women by the p***y. The moderators hounded
Trump continuously as Hillary watched, obviously
trying to hold back her smirks. However, Trump was
smart, his go-to counter-attack was bringing up Bill's
affairs in the Oval office and how Hillary did not handle
the situation very well. Trump also brought along four of
Bill's "women", These women not only accused Mr.
Clinton of sexual assault, but rape.

In this debate, much the same as the last one, the moderators hounded Trump, but turned the cheek for Hillary. As for the issues, Trump focused on border security and the repealing of Obamacare, while Hillary gave vague answers, but we all know she planned to further enable the progressive agenda. Trump also proclaimed that should he win; Hillary Clinton would be in jail. Delusional leftists claimed Trump's remarks to be dictatorial. We get it - enforcing the federal law on American citizens is now sexist, and Hillary is above the law because of her pantsuits and snapchat accounts! Another highlight of the debate was Kenneth Bone. He also goes by the Bone machine or simply Boner. Ken asked the poignant question of "What steps will your energy policy take to meet our energy needs, while at the same time remaining environmentally-friendly and minimizing job loss for fossil power plant workers?" This question launched Kenneth into worldwide stardom. In just weeks he had an advertisement deal with Uber, his own Saturday Night Live sketch, and his very own action figure. Kenneth is a stud and I believe firmly that he voted for Donald Trump.

3RD DEBATE

The 3rd and final debate was held on Wednesday, October 19th at Nevada's UNLV campus. This debate was moderated by Chris Wallace and I will go ahead and say he was the best moderator by far. The debate was very similar to the first. This time it covered 90 minutes into 6 segments with each segment having 15 minutes. Chris Wallace was responsible for each question, and he did a phenomenal job of keeping the candidates in line with the questions and equally pestering BOTH candidates. The topics of the debate were: immigration, Supreme Court picks, economy, debt and entitlements, foreign hot spots, and stamina to be president.

This debate featured the least interruptions and was left to strictly issue talk. Trump spoke passionately against abortion and about the ills of ObamaCare. Supporters say Trump appeared the most presidential in this debate. Oddly enough, Hillary "won" seemingly every poll after the debate. Are Hillary fans just too lazy to get up and vote or do poll pundits only poll Democrats? The world may never know.

26. MAGA3X

In October 2016, project MAGA3X launched.

It began as an informal network of Trump supporters that knew each other from social media, mainly twitter, and was set up initially by Mike Cernovich, Jeff Giesea, Tim Treadstone (street name: Baked Alaska), and myself. We saw it as a project to translate the high energy Trump support online into physical support on the streets, and eventually, votes at the ballot box in swing states to win the election and be the final nail in Hillary Clinton's coffin (electorally speaking, of course).

We identified that there were millions of Trump supporters who wanted to volunteer to help the movement and give them time and energy, but that the RNC was not adequately or effectively supporting the Trump campaign. In the wake of the Trump Tapes release, the RNC had decided that Trump was a lost cause and was not going to win in the general election. They moved their resources and assets to what are called "downticket races" – namely Senate, Governor, Congress, and other races that appear on the election ballot below that of the Presidential race. The RNC decided that since Trump was going to lose, they would cut their losses and go all-in for House and Senate races. We decided that was unacceptable.

We set up MAGA3X on Twitter and Facebook, and created a website. The concept was simple:

Don't just register to vote and vote Trump yourself, get 3 of your friends and family registered and get them to vote for Trump on November 8 too. Just 10 days after launch, the campaign had gotten 24,000 people paying attention on Facebook and done more than 2 million impressions on Twitter.

On October 5th, 2016, I created the following list, drawing on my political campaign experience, and outlined what I thought the most important things MAGA3X could do to assist the Trump campaign:

- Voter Registration (don't forget to make sure YOU are registered)

- Online voter Registration https://ballotpedia.org/Online_voter_registration

- Vote.Gov, Focus on voters in SWING states, If someone moved into a swing state, make sure they register at current address

- Absentee Ballots - https://ballotpedia.org/Absentee_voting

-- we also need to track people who have signed up for this and make sure they mail in returns

- Overseas Voter Registration (Absentee)

- Polling Places: https://gttp.votinginfoproject.org/ (this site is not live yet but will be VERY soon)

MAGA3X only works if we register new voters or bring out people who usually do not vote. 100 million registered voters did not vote in 2012.

State Poll Opening and Closing Times - all times LOCAL

https://ballotpedia.org/State_Poll_Opening_and_Closing
Times(2016)

Targeting polls in swing states (swing polls)

Poll watching - phones, periscope, etc

Exit polling (via tablets)

Car pools to the polls

Run to the polls (vote while you workout)

Coffee and Voting (offer free coffee to our people who come to a certain poll)

Pushing vote by mail (allowed in many states)

Campaigning at the polls -- it is legal to hold Trump signs outside polling locations. Laws vary by state but on average 100ft away is the norm. Usually there will be an areas designated by the local judge of elections.

Inner cities -- these are where the Democrat fraud machinese operate. Might need special ops teams for places like Philly, Richmond, Colombus, Miami

Also, we'd need some kind of war-room, private chat or video chat for E-Day.

In a statement to independent journalist site GotNews, MAGA3X stated:

"MAGA3X was created as a reaction to the

inaction of the GOP in regards to assisting in the election for President of Donald Trump. Reports were streaming in from people who were actively complaining of not getting any support from their local offices. We saw MAGA3X as a Game changer, to assist the Donald Trump campaign's on-ground Voter Outreach on a grassroots level.

It began with the idea of Magnifying and Multiplying individual outreach: Bring Three Trump voters with you on election day. We've expanded the vision to include, doing 3 things that help the campaign on a daily basis, this can be as simple as retweeting, and hashtagging your own tweets with our branded hashtag #MAGA3X."

Mike Cernovich added in a statement on twitter:

"We are at least 40% of the country. We might make up as much as 60%. The hoaxing media for years has run a psyop on the American people, making

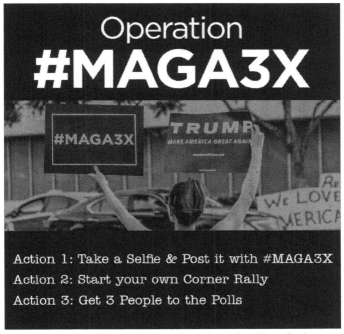

everyone who supporting putting America first feel isolated and alone."

We realized that the best way to find the media's demoralization psyop was to give people a way to join together, to form up, and to be loud and in-your-face about it. We launched the MAGA3X Flash Mobs and recruited team leaders in key swing state cities around the country like Kathy Zhu in Orlando, Florida and Erica Setnick in King of Prussia, PA among so many others. Tim Treadstone led many of the flash mobs, especially in California. We even built a meme generator to promote the meetups, and gave free access to it on our website so that everyone could hold their own meetups, sign waves, counter-protests, rallies, and any other events they wanted to have.

Even left-wing blog Buzzfeed later wrote: The MAGA3X accounts were water cannon of memes,

Breitbart stories, WikiLeaks theories, pro-Trump YouTube videos, and political cartoons, and they swelled to the tens of thousands, eventually gaining

public praise from Gen. Michael Flynn, the national security adviser to President Trump.

Founder Jeff Giesea wrote in a NATO's Defense Strategic Communications Journal in 2015:

"Memetic warfare, as I define it, is competition over narrative, ideas, and social control in a social-media battlefield. One might think of it as a subset of 'information operations' tailored to social media. Information operations involve the collection and dissemination of information to establish a competitive advantage over an opponent. Memetic warfare could also be viewed as a 'digital native' version of psychological warfare, more commonly known as propaganda. If propaganda and public diplomacy are conventional forms of memetic warfare, then trolling and PSYOPs are guerrilla versions. Memetic warfare can be useful at the grand narrative level, at the battle level, or in a special circumstance. It can be offensive, defensive, or predictive. It can be deployed independently or in conjunction with cyber, hybrid, or conventional efforts."

Immediately after the GOP establishment the Hillary Campaign released the Trump Tapes attack video, MAGA3X released a devastating ad about Hillary Clinton. Videos and images of Hillary Clinton, Bill Clinton and their various rape victims played in silence with the words superimposed: "What kind of person would stay married to a rapist? Lie for a rapist? Cover up for a rapist? Attack the victims of rape? Threaten the victims of rape? Laugh about maligning a 12-year old rape victim? But say that victims deserve to be believed? Seriously, what kind of person? Someone who cares only about power. And thinks you're stupid enough to give it to her." These images were juxtaposed with images of Hillary and Bill's victims: Juanita Broadderick and Kathy Shelton.

We realized that the best way to cut through the media psyop that there were no Trump supporters was to have flash mobs of spontaneous Trump groups popping up all over the country, and sharing them via social media so no one would be able to cover it up – there was no way to hide the fact that thousands of people were holding these massive flash mobs in totally disparate areas of the country. After the MAGA3X flash mobs began, the RNC began to get upset that people were more interested in going to our events and meetups than go to work for downticket races. The grassroots wanted to help Trump, because the movement was behind him and the country, not just any candidate that happened to have an R next to their name. We received reports that RNC leaders were discouraging people from going to MAGA3X rallies, and telling them to not support us. We responded via livestream and twitter, as covered by many blogs, that our efforts were designed to support Donald Trump for President and not any other campaigns, but that we welcomed other campaigns to come and join us. I personally travelled to flash mobs in Philadelphia, Hershey, Orlando, Miami, Ohio, Virginia, Maryland, New York, Boston, Maine, Los Angeles, and Huntington Beach, California.

The night before the election, we held a flash mob at Independence Hall, Philadelphia, outside a rally held by Hillary Clinton, Bill Clinton, Chelsea Clinton,

Barack Obama, and Michelle Obama. They were all there. We decided they couldn't just take over our city unanswered. We got 30 people to the flash mob, right in the heart of one of the most liberal cities in the country. Interestingly, most of the people who came to the rally were from New Jersey, coming to see Bon Jovi and Bruce Springsteen who each only played one song. It was a characteristically tone-deaf move from the Hillary campaign, bringing the completely wrong artists to turn out a Philly crowd. After the rally, I live-streamed thousands of cars driving across the Ben Franklin Bridge back into New Jersey. This was the first time I realized that Philadelphia might not come out to vote for Hillary on November 8th.

On election day, MAGA3X launched the only pro-Trump 24/7 livestreaming news network via our YouTube channel. We created a framework for the only national and international source of pro-Trump breaking news and street journalism in the world. We called in MAGA3X TV, an ad hoc live stream anchored by major social media influencers and supported by producers who assist with technology and gathering research. Since so much information was being dumped in the lead up to the election, and the mainstream media was doing a terrible job at dissecting and disseminating the information to the voters, we decided to bypass the sluggish Old Media and take this crucial information directly from the source and bring them to concerned Trump supporters. We monitored Twitter, Facebook, and Instagram, and sent people into the field where mainstream media refused to go. We created a platform with the ability to have live "hosts" in-studio, as well as pulling in correspondents in the field on Election Day, like myself in Philadelphia via Periscope, and many others around the country. This way, we beat the Old Media at their own game, showing the truth to our viewers faster and more efficiently than any other platform on Election Day 2016.

One of our top advisors, James Brower, conducted a social media analysis of MAGA3X following the election. He found the hashtag to be a major trend across Twitter, Facebook, and Instagram in the final 220 hours of the election, with significant numbers concentrated in Florida, Pennsylvania, Texas, Louisiana, and California. Overall, in the last 220 hours of the election, MAGA3X garnered more than 26 million impressions. Targeted in key states, this effort absolutely had a significant effect on Trump's victory. It was able to cut through the media psyop that Trump voters were isolated and alone, and showed them that there were thousands of like-minded Trump supporters, right in their own local areas. These meetups were so successful and the bonds created between supporters so strong, that many have taken on a life of their own even after the election. As of March 2017, MAGA3X is still receiving roughly 1 million impressions per day, and is tweeted out hundreds of times daily. Discussions are currently underway to determine how to move forward with this energy, but one thing is certain, MAGA3X, in whatever form it takes, will definitely be a force to be reckoned with in 2018 and 2020. The revolution continues...

25: STOP THE STEAL

In October 2016, as the race entered its final days, Citizens for Trump partnered with Roger Stone to take part in 'Operation - Stop The Steal'. The goal of this operation was to combat vote fraud and election rigging. There were two main focuses of the operation. First, a volunteer-led exit poll. Second, cyber security of the voting machines themselves.

Across all the groups involved, Stop the Steal succeeded in recruiting over 7,000 poll workers nationwide. The goal of these workers was two-fold. They were to stand outside polls and conduct an exit survey of voter preferences. Then, they were to count the number of voters that turned out to vote at that precinct. While performing this voluntary survey, all members were trained to be non-partisan, refrain from wearing any pro-candidate clothing or paraphernalia (such as the MAGA red hats), and to be sure to comply with any and all state regulations regarding volunteering at the polls. They would conduct scientifically valid, methodologically sound exit polls outside certain targeted precinct polling places in eight swing states. Our volunteers were trained to take scientifically based exit polls to help determine whether or not the final totals reported from voting machines reflected the actual vote.

Many news organizations join together to conduct a joint exit poll in the US, called the National Election Pool (NEP Poll). This consists of ABC, AP, CBS, CNN, FOX News, and NBC. While they may announce the results as "CNN Exit Poll Results," they are actually reading from the same poll. Since 2004, this exit poll has been conducted for the mainstream media by Edison Media Research. In designing Stop the Steal, all parameters and best practices of the NEP Poll were studied and taken into consideration. Furthering the case for the necessity of accurate exit polls, the US State Department under Hillary Clinton required not more than a 2 percent deviance between actual reported results and exit poll results in judging the integrity of foreign elections. It would seem only fair that the US ought to be held to the same standard by which it judged foreign countries.

After the way the mainstream media had treated Team Trump over the previous year, there was little trust in their ability to accurately conduct and report exit polls fairly. In fact, media agencies had been under much criticism in 2012 and 2008 for reporting exit polls early, in many cases even before states had finished voting. This had an adverse effect on turnout and gave the false impression that the election had, in fact, ended, and so people would stay home rather than heading to the polls.

Like nothing else during the 2016 campaign season, Stop the Steal had the mainstream media and the left roiled. It's like we touched a nerve or something. George Patton once said, 'when you're taking the most flack, you know you're right over the target.' Dozens of fake news articles were written about our operations, completely invented fictitious methods and plans that we were supposedly going to implement. The general theme of the media smear campaign was that Stop the Steal volunteers were going to be intimidating voters by approaching them before (not after) they voted or went into the polls in order to suppress votes. Nothing could be further from the truth, as we had not instructed anyone to even talk to voters prior to voting. The entire point was an exit poll to be conducted following vote-casting, not before, and for all volunteers to be non-partisan and impartial. Evidentially that was not enough of a story for the Huffington Post, so they decided to cook one up about us intimidating voters in order to suppress Hillary support.

As a side note here, it's funny how these fake news reports about yet-to-occur voter intimidation created so much news controversy, yet in 2008, video evidence of armed Black Panthers actually preventing voters from entering a polling place in Philadelphia resulted in no charges, no investigation, and no reporting from mainstream media. The infamous video was actually captured by one of my Election Day College Republican volunteers in Philadelphia. I had expected arrests and upheaval to occur. I soon learned that while the right is held to a standard, the left has none.

In October 2016, the Democrat Party sued Stop the Steal in Pennsylvania, Ohio, Arizona, and Nevada. Roger Stone was sued, and I was named as a co-

conspirator in the lawsuit. We were sued under the Ku Klux Klan Act of 1871, which was preposterous, as neither Roger nor I are registered Democrats.

Federal judges ruled for the Democrats in the first round, issuing a restraining order to block Stop the Steal operations in those states. Soon after, on November 4, 2016, the 6th Circuit Court of Appeals stayed the restraining order, allowing the volunteer program to move forward. The 6th Circuit found that the Democrats did not have enough, or actually any factual evidence to back up their wild and spurious allegations. Finally, the US Supreme Court was appealed to by David Boyce, a top DNC attorney. The Supreme Court, too, struck it down on the same grounds of baselessness. After that, we could then proudly say that Stop the Steal was a US Supreme Court-Approved Exit Poll Survey. Thanks, Dems!

On Election Day, Stop the Steal operated in realtime, with volunteer data input and broadcast directly on StopTheSteal.com. The program was found to be highly accurate in the end, especially in PA, OH, and FL. It success can be duplicated in any race, at any level, and will be an effective tool in the 2018 midterm elections, and Donald Trump's re-election in 2020.

It was our assessment that Stop The Steal's relentless push for poll workers stationed outside key areas thwarted plans by the Hillary camp and local party machines to stuff ballots, file fraudulent absentee ballots (such as in Broward County, FL), and even front-load votes cast on election day voting machines (more on that in a later chapter). This would later be proven when Jill Stein attempted to mount a recount of Pennsylvania, but was stopped by, again, complete lack of evidence.

On the other Election Day operation (EDO) side, we worked with the Trump campaign to put together cyber task forces comprised of both lawyers and techs. We combined the best election law experts with cyber security experts, many with US military special operations background. These cyber task forces volunteered their time for Mr. Trump, and freely gave their efforts to uphold the election process in key areas of key states. While numerous inconsistencies and discrepancies were highlighted by election watchers, the cyber task forces stepped up and fought election rigging. To my knowledge, they even found, in Philadelphia, several hacked voting machines even before Election Day began. These machines were duly reported to all local Boards of Election, and in many cases had their microchips reset, or the machines themselves were impounded before the election took place.

With Mr. Trump shining a light early on about the possibility of corruption, vote stealing, and election-rigging, thousands of Americans put their time, effort, and special skills to work for the movement. This, to me, will always represent one of the most powerful aspects of the Trump movement – no one asked to be paid, no one asked to be recognized. They only asked to be heard.

26: NOVEMBER 8, 2016

On the morning of November 8th, I set out to position myself where I thought I would be most effective for Mr. Trump on Election Day. As elections go, the political campaign is basically ended the night before votes are cast. At that point, people have decided whether to vote or not, absentee ballots have been mailed, and voters have largely decided by that point which candidate they will support. Random acts may cause disruptions in voting patterns, and misinformation can have some effect on turnout (like mainstream exit polls or Ted Cruz' chicanery in Iowa). The correct mindset to maintain on Election Day is legality.

Elections are tricky things, and shenanigans can take place at any point before, during, or after polls are opened. Numerous election law complexities must be understood and followed, and many people are involved: official election workers, poll watchers, campaigns, police, poll volunteers, and most importantly the voters themselves. At any point in the process, there are various channels for fraud and misconduct. With these thoughts in mind, I decided to plant myself in the place that was known to be rife with Election Day incidents year after year, in a state where Trump was on the cusp of winning, and a place I knew like the back of my hand. I took to the streets of my hometown, Philadelphia.

That morning, the thought was that there would be no bigger upset than if the Democrat stronghold of Pennsylvania tipped in Trump's favor. Pennsylvania had not been won by a Republican candidate since 1988. Having been involved with the Bush, McCain, and

Romney campaigns, I knew that the Keystone State was never seriously sought by Republican candidates. The recurring line among political operatives was "Pennsylvania is Fool's Gold for Republicans" – a line I heard many times when attempting to deploy political funds and focus to PA. Despite a few late polls that had PA at 50-50, Trump was not expected to win it, and Democrat campaign workers are willing to do just about anything to keep that from happening.

I took to the polls in Philadelphia with my iPhone and my Periscope account, linked to Twitter. There, I uncovered all kinds of illegal behavior at the polls, from electioneering to threats of physical violence against myself and others. In the first poll I stopped by, in North Philadelphia just steps from my alma mater Temple University, a Democrat was caught campaigning for Hillary inside the polling place. On my video (still posted on my Periscope account) you can hear a woman urging, "We need your votes," while someone else can be heard trying to hush her up with "Shh, shh!!!"

To believe that I just happened upon the singular, sole incidence of nefarious behavior would be nothing short of willful ignorance – and believe me, my luck isn't that good. Instead, I found illegal activity all over as I made my way though the City of Brotherly Love.

At one point, police were called when an official, appointed Republican poll worker was threatened with a belt by a Hillary-supporting judge of elections. Joseph Defelice, Pennsylvania's GOP Chairman said the Democrats were banning Republican poll watchers and minority inspectors.

"They're saying, 'We don't want you here. We don't have Republicans in here. We're full already. I don't know what that piece of paper is. This happened in 2012. We made a big issue out of this," Defelice said. I was following local political and news accounts on Twitter, and a few postings alerted me to the potential violence in Northeast Philadelphia. I hopped into my car and headed across town to the scene of the incident.

Arriving, I found it to be a poll held in a union hall in Northeast Philadelphia. Outside, the hall had Democrat political paraphernalia posted all over the walls and doors - a clear violation of Pennsylvania's 10-ft from the doors regulation on electioneering. Indeed, the Judge of Elections was joking around with Democrat poll workers, while the lone Republican was forced outside of the spaces, despite having a court-approved poll watching certificate. He had been told, by the official Judge of Elections that he would "take off his belt and beat you" if the poll watcher did not leave the building.

I asked what could have caused an election official to speak that way to a poll watcher, and he explained that when the polls opened, there were already votes registered on one of the machines. This was a clear violation of election law, and a further worry about potential rigging of electronic voting machines. If this could happen to one machine in Philadelphia, it surely could have happened to many more. I sent word to my liaison with the Trump cyber task forces operating in

Philadelphia and other key cities to be on the lookout for the tactic.

Once the Judge of Elections saw me, he asked who I was and what I was doing there. I identified myself, and showed him my own certificate as a lawfully court-appointed poll watcher. I kept my phone on the entire time, with Periscope rolling. Unedited live broadcasts are the ultimate equalizer, because all they can show is exactly what is going on in real-time. They cannot be altered and they cannot be faked. Periscope, Facebook Live, and now YouTube Live, are the greatest weapons in the growing arsenal of citizen journalism. Failing to realize this, the Judge of Elections threw me out as well. By the end of the day, we had taken him to court, and had the election machine with fraudulent votes impounded. We cited my Periscope as evidence. Be careful!

After my reporting on the Northeast Philadelphia Judge of Elections reached the Gateway Pundit and Drudge Report, a Huffington Post reporter traveled to interview him. On tape, he admitted he threatened a poll watcher with a belt:

Working with my friends at PhillyGOP, we shared many instances of Voter Fraud and Voter Intimidation in the city:

- "My name is Brittany Foreman... and today I witnessed Voter Fraud." #VoterFraud ILLEGAL. Please SHARE

 Philly GOP
@PhillyGOP

Following

"My name is Brittany Foreman... and today I witnessed Voter Fraud." #VoterFraud ILLEGAL. Please SHARE

- Video of poll watcher Earl Markey from 48/2 telling story of how he was intimidated and left the polling place. https://twitter.com/PhillyGOP/status/796094 240937955328

- 52nd ward 15th div Democratic Commiteeman allowed to hang out inside poll, say "hey remember you are Democrats" - Election judge allows it https://twitter.com/PhillyGOP/status/796111 744741572608

- photo a poll watcher took at 49-6 - there's a note on the back of piece of paper at the table that reads, "Son voted in place of father." https://twitter.com/PhillyGOP/status/796111 744741572608

- 56th ward 1st division - Electionnering on the inside - went in the booth with voter. https://twitter.com/PhillyGOP/status/796076 753651437569

- Court-appointed Minority Inspector at 17&Spring Garden: "I was just told...I'm not allowed to be in the room & ... to wait outside". ILLEGAL

The day was only getting started. Joe Defelice, the Philadelphia GOP Chairman took the media early in the day to expose the fact that Democrats were banning Republican poll watchers and minority inspectors . "They're just not letting them inside.

They're either poll watchers or minority inspectors. Minority inspectors are court appointed whereas poll watchers are mandated through the city to be inside that polling place," Defelice said. "They're saying, 'We don't want you here. We don't have Republicans in here. We're full already. I don't know what that piece of paper is.' This happened in 2012. We made a big issue out of this."

Online sources also reported that day that Clinton supporters had been caught on camera committing voter fraud outside a polling station in Philadelphia by encouraging people to vote for the Democrat Party. Footage showed two African-American men handing out campaign material within feet of a polling station encouraging voters to "push button number 1" to voter for the Democrats. The material is "paid for by the Democratic County". Voter intimidation and rigging was not isolated to Philadelphia. Dozens of stories came in from across Pennsylvania, and from other big swing states like Ohio and Florida.

In Broward County Florida, according to a former Secretary of Elections Department employee, there was a secret room where Democrat insiders filled out ballots for Hillary Clinton. An affidavit filed by Chelsey Marie Smith accused election officials of filling out blank absentee ballots to officials who she saw filling the ballots out at the Supervisor of Elections headquarters. County Supervisor Brenda Snipes claimed staff were "replicating damaged ballots." Smith reported the fake ballots to be in the thousands, and that the operation had been going on for weeks before the election. Nearly 180,000 mail-in votes were not legally counted. As of this writing, Snipes continues to supervise elections, despite her numerous legal issues and court appearances due to her mishandling of election law.

Back in Philadelphia, I spent the rest of the day travelling to areas of the city and periscoping or Facebook Live-streaming the streets.

At one poll location not far from my old apartment in West Philadelphia, I saw a man wearing a Hillary shirt standing at the front door, holding it open and talking to people as they went inside. Knowing this was in violation of election law, I walked over and began filming. The man identified himself as a Hillary volunteer, and began screaming at me to leave and threatened me with physical assault. When I asked him why, he called me a Nazi and said I was intimidating voters. He then ran out into the street screaming "Nazi Nazi Nazi Nazi." I should mention, that I was not wearing anything partisan at the time, only a faded blue jacket and a pair of cargo pants. Other Hillary volunteers then told me that I was breaking the law by filming on a public street. I reminded them that the Supreme Court has ruled that taking photographs and filming things that are plainly visible from public spaces (such as sidewalks) is protected under the First Amendment. They did not appreciate that, and became quite belligerent towards me. Check out my live feeds if you want to see any of this, as I am sure mainstream media "fact checkers" will dispute this (and just about every other page of this book).

Throughout the day, I had been listening to reports on the ground of turnout from around the country, and focusing on a few bellweather counties in each of the swing states. Pennsylvania was my main focus, but Florida and Colorado were also on my radar. Prior to election day, we already knew Ohio was confirmed in the win column and that Virginia was likely a bridge too far. (Trump became the first Republican since Calvin Coolidge in 1924 to win without carrying Virginia.) In Pennsylvania, things were looking good. Interestingly, early on in the day, I noticed a large amount of turnout in the west and central parts of the state, and a somewhat smaller turnout where I was in the southeastern suburbs and the city of Philadelphia. The old joke about Pennsylvania politics is that the state is Philadelphia, Pittsburgh and Kentucky in the middle – two liberal cities and a conservative center. I spent the day conversing with many pro-Trump political operatives, including the great Adam Gingrich. I had other people check my math to make sure I wasn't seeing things, and many of them agreed that it was solid. At 5:10pm on Election Day, I tweeted: If current turnout holds we win Pennsylvania. By that point, I knew things were moving in our direction, but I had to be sure. Pennsylvania had not gone for a Republican in 28 years, and even though most elections it would come close, it simply never materialized. Lots of people had told me to forget about PA, to go focus on other, more winnable states, that it wasn't going to happen. Thing is, I've got a wicked stubborn streak in me, and its even worse when I know I'm right.

I've worked in campaigns on over two dozen Election Days, both primaries and generals. Election Days usually follow a certain pattern. There's an early rush of voters hitting the ballots on their way to work from around 7-9am, then a thinner, but steady stream from about 9-Noon, an uptick around lunchtime, totally dead from around 2-4pm, and then the after-work rush. From 5pm until 8pm when polls close is typically the largest bloc of voters, when the long lines are reported, and can lead to the most irregularities. This time of day can make or break an election, and can even see more voters turn out than all other times of the day put together. So, with that knowledge, I waited to see what Philadelphia had in store for Trump and Clinton.

In short, there was nothing.

(Center City Philadelphia, Nov 8, 6pm)

For two hours, I drove around Philadelphia

livestreaming and reporting progress the entire time, looking for signs of lines, after-work turnout, families taking their kids to see what the election process was like, and found nothing. I had made a list of the biggest polls in each ward of the city, and divided them up by geography. Some places have multiple divisions voting at one location, such as Samuel Fels High School in Northeast Philadelphia which has 4 divisions. I drove into West Philly, then down past Philadelphia Community College, South Philly, Center City – and the lines were simply not there. It was a ghost town.

At Temple University, my own alma mater, there were long lines, but I did not see that as significant, because turnout had been down there all day. It's a scientific fact that college students don't do anything before 2pm.

(South Philly, Nov 8, 6:30pm)

I started to get excited. If Philadelphia wasn't turning out, and the West and Central parts of Pennsylvania did, that meant Trump would win the state. If Trump won Pennsylvania, plus Ohio, plus Florida, that meant he was going to win the presidency. I decided there wasn't much more I could do in Philadelphia, and decided to go where the election was coming to its final end – New York City. Both Trump and Clinton were holding their victory parties there. One would end in celebration, the other in pure madness.

I sped over to Philadelphia's 30th Street Station, threw on my MAGA3X t-shirt, covered it with a suit jacket that was hung in the back of my car (you learn to live out of your car on campaigns), and double-timed it to the lobby. I made sure to grab a few phone battery packs and extra chargers – the lifeblood of anyone trying to work in the field here in the 21st century. I pulled up the app on my iPhone and at 7:44pm purchased a one-way ticket on the 8:01pm train to New York City for forty-nine dollars and fifty cents. I ran into the gift shop and purchased my usual traveling fare – 2 Coke Zeroes and a protein bar. Shooting down the escalator, I managed to plop into my seat on the train just as it pulled out into the night and streaked north through the chill November air towards the final victory. I laughed that I was now literally on the Trump Train.

Apple had just pushed the buggy iOS10 a few weeks before, and Twitter was even glitchier than usual. For the first time, I tried downloading a third-party app to access it. I tried a few different ones before settling on Echofan – it was free, and the ads sucked, but it wasn't freezing or stick, it worked. I scrolled through a few account lists I had set up of political operatives, breaking news, and press polls attached to the candidates. Lots of text messages and calls were coming into my phone, but I barely had time to respond to any of them. People were starting to get worried about Florida, I remember, but I tweeted out that the conservative Panhandle had yet to be counted – liberal cities always report their vote results first. As I read through information gushing in from around the country, I nodded in an out of consciousness. I had only slept about 2 hours in the previous three days. I decided to take a power nap, a light sleep for 15-20 minutes, the same tactic that had gotten me through college and the military.

We pulled in to New York's Penn Station, and I trekked up to street level, the bright lights of Madison Square Garden shining above me. I looked up and saw the Empire State Building and blinked when I saw a giant Donald Trump staring back at me. At first I thought I was totally losing it. I rubbed my eyes and looked again. Trump was still there. I realized the building's LED lights had been rigged up to display images of the candidates as different states were called for one or the other. Trump had just won Ohio, I learned, hopping into an Uber. I received a text from a source, "Clinton people who don't even smoke are smoking right now. Unreal."

I got out at the Hilton Midtown and checked in to the party. Outside on the street, dump trucks and first responder vehicles protected the partygoers, along with a mix of police and federal agents. The tireless Josh Macias of Veterans for Trump had arranged for me to get on the list, he himself had decided to stay behind in his home state of Virginia in hopes that he could swing Old Dominion towards Trump. Inside, I greeted a few friends and turned down offered drinks, myself sober for 11 years. Looking around, though, I had to admit I felt it was bittersweet. I was surrounded by 20-something Trump staffers and interns in suits, top donors to the campaign in well-heeled shoes and dresses, as well as the usual assortment of media types covering the event. The members of the press had lost their characteristic smugness, and all looked like they wanted to hit the bar.

Around midnight, I decided to step outside the hotel and take a look at what was going on around the streets of New York at that point. Directly out front, I found exactly what I wanted. About 50 Trump supporters with red MAGA hats, homemade signs, and American flags were going wild, cheering and screaming how excited they were for Trump. I ran over to them, where the NYPD had erected metal barricades to protect the revelers. I ran over, hopped the barricade, and threw up my fist. I had no idea who they were, but one look at my MAGA had and, "Trump! Trump! Trump! Trump!" everyone chanted. The crowd was as diverse as any Trump rally, despite what the mainstream media will tell you, and you can go back on my livestreams to see it.

Teenagers, moms, dads, every ethnicity, every background – it was definitely a Manhattan crowd. I spent the next few hours out there, giving a few interviews to international media that had set up outside our barricades. Every time a new state was called for Trump on the Empire State Building, we all cheered. I laughed when someone yelled "We won Texas!" – the idea the media and the Left had been pushing that Texas was somehow in play was one of the dumbest ploys of the entire year. Of course Trump won Texas – and won by a million votes.

As the night grew longer, not one of us lost energy, but we were getting more and more impatient with the media refusing to call states for Trump, even when nearly 99% of vote results were entered. At 1:36am, the AP finally called Pennsylvania for Trump, confirming what I had reported nearly 8 hours earlier. I headed back over toward the hotel to see if anyone had any idea what was going on, but no one could make sense of it. Many operatives started have their constant fear of the 2000 recount creep back up, and a few even texted me that I had better get ready to pack my bags for Harrisburg. Standing outside the hotel, I was watching a CNN feed on a tiny tv in the side of a firetruck that had been stationed on the sidewalk. At 2:05am, creepy John Podesta took the stage at the Hillary event and basically said "Several states are too close to call, so we're not going to have anything more to say tonight."

Reports would later come out that Hillary could not physically take the stage at that point, and had flown into an uncontrollable rage and dumped water on at least one assistant. Secret Service officers told at least one source that she began yelling, screaming obscenities, and pounding furniture. She picked up objects and threw them at attendants and staff, in an uncontrollable rage, much like she had at many times during her time in the White House. Her aides would not allow her to come out in public. She supposedly screamed, "If that f***ing b*****d wins, we all hang from nooses! If I lose, it's all on your heads for screwing this up!" She was then carried to her medical van by her security team, and may have been sedated.

After Podesta left stage, a ripple went through the security officials around me. I looked up from my phone to see dozens of officers and agents take lines in two echelons on the sidewalk, facing each other. Senior agents ran around talking into earpieces and walkie-talkies. I didn't need to ask what was going on, but I wanted to stay and see for myself. No other invitees were outside the hotel ,and suddenly in the middle of Manhattan, with the eyes of the entire world seemingly on us, it was silent. You could hear a pin drop 6th Avenue. The air crackled with electricity.

One NYPD officer leaned in toward me and said, "He's coming."

"Who?" I asked.

"The President," he responded with a smile. At 2:20am Donald Trump walked out of a black SUV with his senior staff and advisors and walked right past us. Every officer lining the street saluted him as they passed and headed into the hotel.

Trump saluted back and smiled, "Thanks for staying up for us," he joked, with the officers laughing.

Trump entered the main entrance of the hotel to give his victory speech, and the officers broke ranks. The one I'd talked to looked back over at me and said, "Things are gonna get better."

"Why's that?" I asked.

He gave me a quick nod and replied in a no-nonsense tone, "We got Trump now."

27: BASED REALITY

According to Wikipedia "Reality is the state of things as they actually exist, rather than as they may appear or might be imagined. Reality includes everything that is and has been, whether or not it is observable or comprehensible. A still broader definition includes that which has existed, exists, or will exist".

There were two races for president in 2016. I don't mean two presidential campaigns, Trump vs Clinton; I mean two completely separate races. To anyone who has read the great Scott Adams, they will be familiar with the concept of corporate-owned media, also known as mainstream media, ensconced in cable news and national print media, portrayed one reality, meanwhile independent media, found on social media and conservative news sites, showed another.

In the world of the mainstream media, the election was a cakewalk for Hillary Clinton, and an endless stream of gaffes for Donald Trump. Their narrative was that she was the inevitable winner right from the start, almost pre-ordained to the presidency. To them, Donald Trump was the result of a massive temper tantrum, and represented exactly the kind of racism, sexism, and backwards-thinking that Hillary and progressives are always blaming for everything wrong in America.

In the world of independent media (citizen media), the election was seen as a struggle between a powerful corporate establishment hell-bent on globalizing the world to turn national citizens into bland consumers, and a movement to restore traditional American values. To them, Hillary Clinton was the embodiment of collusion between Wall Street, OPEC, and crypto-communism that they saw as the core issues of everything wrong in America.

See how that works?

The way Scott Adams described it was that it's like one group of people watching two different movies at the same time, but movies with the same characters. In one movie, Donald Trump was the monstrous villain, and in the other movie, Hillary was the evil gorgon-queen. Instead of a movie theater, this increasingly played out on the internet, with Facebook and Twitter being some of the main fields of battle. How many likes, shares, and retweets could this article get? Which hashtags were trending? How could either side break through to the other narrative?

Stories like Hillary's health, Wiki-leaks, Benghazi, and the Clinton Foundation's cornucopia of corruption were barely given a moment's breath in mainstream sources. In contrast, these stories formed the backbone of social media discussion and inquiry. The blackout of information or airtime given to these topics helped reinforce the perception on social media that the establishment was putting its thumb on the scale of public opinion going into the election.

Rather than allow news and events to act as a fulcrum in the election, and people deciding how they felt about the two candidates, the establishment instead colluded to portray one candidate (Clinton) as infallible, and the other candidate (Trump) as unelectable. This led to an amplification of stories about Trump's past business dealings, legal tax practices, and a litany of supposed personal scandals, all of which were eventually proven false. In the same vein, almost none of either reality's negative stories about the opposing candidate found their way into the other side. Instead of debating stories on their merits, it began a process by which news outlets, reporters, and the use of unnamed sources was called into question. The mainstream media outlets abandoned all semblances of journalistic standards as each competed obsessively for a mythical goal: the story that would be the end of Trump.

It never happened, because it didn't exist.

Instead, the media turned into the Boy Who Cried Wolf, with more and more stories by mainstream sources proven outright to be false, or overblown controversies turning out to be much more smoke than fire. This drove many to lose faith in mainstream outlets, something that going into 2016 was not exactly seen as the paragons of truth and honesty. Meanwhile, stories trending on social media were either ignored or poo-pooed by the bicoastal elite, not realizing how much traction they were picking up with Americans who has increasingly grown distrustful of Big Media and Big Government.

With two groups of people watching the same movie, there was only going to be one ending. It's like watching a mystery and you think one person is the killer, but it was really the person standing next to you the whole time. There could be only one ending. Instead of a competition between rival campaigns, 2016 became a contest between rival realities.

So, which one was real? How do we figure out which one was the actual reality? There is a theory subscribed to by some physicists and web developers called the "mass simulation theory" which is kind of like the movie *The Matrix*. Their point is, essentially, that there is no way to prove that we are not all living in a simulated reality, and they believe there is evidence that we actually are. The term they used to differentiate that from actual existence is "based reality." They think we are living in a simulation. "There's a billion-to-one chance we're living in based reality," said Elon Musk, June 2016.

Whether we are living in the Matrix or not, Trump reality is definitely Based Reality.

In this case, there was a social experiment conducted shortly after the election that inadvertently showed the disparity between the realities, by the theater department at NYU. They decided to conduct a restaging of the third debate between Trump and Clinton, but switch their genders. They had a female actor play Trump and a male actor play Clinton. All words, gestures, body language, and tone were replicated verbatim to the candidates. The man acted like Hillary and the woman acted like Trump.

The NYU professors began the project with a hypothesis: They assumed that Trump's "aggression"— his tendency to interrupt and attack—would never be tolerated in a woman, and that Clinton's "competence and preparedness" would seem even more convincing coming from a man. Their pro-Hillary bias assumed that people only voted for Trump because he was a man and disliked Hillary because she was a woman.

What happened to them popped a huge hole in their reality. They suddenly started noticing things they never had before. Some questions that arose were, "What was Clinton smiling about all the time?" And "Didn't she seem a little stiff, tethered to rehearsed statements at the podium, while Trump, plainspoken and confident, freely roamed the stage? Which one would audiences find more likeable?" One professor remarked "People across the board were surprised that their expectations about what they were going to experience were upended."

NYU audience-members, all Hillary supporters, were equally perplexed and mesmerized. "We heard a lot of "now I understand how this happened"—meaning how Trump won the election. People got upset. There was a guy two rows in front of me who was literally holding his head in his hands, and the person with him was rubbing his back. The simplicity of Trump's message became easier for people to hear when it was coming from a woman—that was a theme."

"One person said, "I'm just so struck by how precise Trump's technique is." Another—a musical theater composer —said that Trump created "hummable lyrics," while Clinton talked a lot, and everything she said was true and factual, there was no "hook" to it. Someone said that the male Hillary Clinton was "really punchable" because of all the unnecessary smiling. And a lot of people were just very surprised by the way it upended their expectations about what they thought they would feel or experience. There was someone who described the female Donald Trump as his Jewish aunt who would take care of him, even though he might not like his aunt. Someone else described her as the middle school principal who you don't like, but you know is doing good things for you.

In the end, one professor noted "It gave me an understanding of what people heard and experienced when Trump spoke" and why people had voted for Trump during the election. He realized that he was watching the wrong movie all along. While neither of the professors admitted it, its clear that it was their overwhelming desire to see a female president that made them overlook all of Hillary's many flaws, while overlooking anything positive about Trump and overblowing anything the least bit negative about him.

While this certainly isn't the first time that cognitive dissonance has played a role in how people view elections, 2016 may have been the most stark. People tend to overemphasize information that confirms their bias, and dismiss information that contrasts with their bias. In effect, reality dissonance (or even reality fraud) played a huge role in how many in the mainstream media called the election, and gave rise to headlines like "Clinton Has a 98% Chance of Winning" only to have her lose hours later.

Interestingly enough, the idea of a Hillary Clinton presidency, something supposedly "in-the-works" for 40 years, has now been consigned to the realm of science fiction. There have been novels written in the past about what would happen if she'd won, and there may be more movies and novels yet to be written about it, but they will always remain alternate histories, and never come true. We will never know what reality would be like with Hillary Clinton as Commander-In-Chief.

Even now as I write this some months after the campaign, millions have yet to accept the reality they live in as true. That dissonance and general feeling that "Hillary should have won" will form the basis for the anti-Trump movement as he moves into the 2018 midterms and 2020 re-election phase. Don't be surprised if the Democrats end up choosing someone extremely "Trumpian" to challenge the incumbent president.

28: THE CHRISTIAN VOTE

Many pundits and political operatives assured themselves that there was no way Donald Trump would be able to win Christians. They said his highly-publicized playboy lifestyle from the 90s, his multiple marriages and his less-than-stellar record of Scripture knowledge would disqualify him from winning the support of the religious right, a key constituency for any Republican candidate. Furthermore, Christians represent over 80% of American voters overall, an unassailable fact of American politics. How could someone like Donald Trump ever win them? The path was simple. He asked for their support. He worked for their support. Donald Trump did not campaign by saying he was the greatest Christian, but he promised to protect Christians, and Christianity in the American sphere. After 8 years of feeling under assault by the actions of President Barack Obama, Christians were looking for a candidate to protect the free practice of their faith, as guaranteed by the U.S. Constitution.

In the end, Mr. Trump won 1 in 4 evangelical voters, and 55% of regular church-going Christians. In the primaries, he won states like South Carolina, Louisiana, Arkansas, and Missouri where evangelicals are a large portion of the vote. At the same time, Senator Ted Cruz had positioned himself as the true Christian conservative in the race. Supporters of Cruz had become particularly hostile to Trump supporters during the primary and often pointed to their Christian faith as the reason for their vehement objection to Trump.

So, how can Trump's overwhelming Christian support be explained? I will post here one of the best long-form writings I have seen on the subject. It was an anonymous post on a personal blog that has since been deleted.

Fortunately, the internet never forgets.

I present it unedited. If you ever wanted to understand how this happened and how Trump-supporting Christians think, you'll want to read this. If you don't care about it, then maybe this isn't the chapter for you. Feel free to skip ahead and continue living in your world of ignorance!

"To The "Never Trumper"- A Biblical Case For Trump"

It is my estimation that 90% of the people who clicked on this link did so to openly mock and ridicule the redneck, Biblically illiterate, idiot who would dare to put the words, "Bible" and "Trump" in the same sentence. If this is you, congratulations to me for getting you to read this article, and congratulations to you because I am neither an idiot nor a heretic. The following is not some poorly-patched together theological treatise that attempts to warp the Word of God in order to justify my political sacrilege.

But since I've got you reading, let's make a wager shall we? You read this article all the way through and as Cruz said, allow your "conscience" to be swayed, or not swayed, by what I believe to be Biblical wisdom. You have the right to judge for yourself.

I fit the classic profile of a "Never Trumper." I am a highly educated, staunchly theologically and politically conservative pastor's wife, who plans to one day homeschool her children. I even want to be a "Never Trumper." I really do. It sounds so principled, so brave, to be a political nonconformist who refuses to buckle under the weight of societal temptation, or fall under the spell of the big mouthed billionaire with his lofty promises for a better future. I CANNOT, however, allow myself to ignore the principles laid out in the Word of God for situations such as the political debacle Americans have unfortunately found themselves in.

In Luke 9, we find the disciples recovering from a serious blow to their pride. Despite their best combined efforts, they had been unable to drive a demon out of a troubled young man, and had been reprimanded by Christ for their lack of faith. Just a few verses later, we find the dejected 12 incensed that another man, an outsider, was able to do what they had not. I believe Jesus' surprising answer to their protests has great ramifications for today's political conundrum.

Verses 49-50 reads: 'Master,' said John, 'we saw a man driving out demons in Your name and we tried to stop him, because he is not one of us.' 'Do not stop him,' Jesus said, 'for whoever is not against you is for you.'

I can sense your hackles immediately rising from across the screen. "But Trump is NOT for us!" you object, "his essence oozes the opposite of Christian values!" I would first ask you to remember that we are NOT electing Trump to a sacred or ecclesiastical office. We are electing him to a political office. If this was a question of placing Trump in charge of my church or Christian organization, you would have to hogtie and hold me down in order to get me to vote for him. I am not arguing for Trump's morality here.

I am simply stating that in this specific office, as President, he has gone to great lengths to demonstrate that he will protect and champion the rights of the American evangelical if he were to be elected, even if he does not personally embrace those values. I would think that his promise to appoint a conservative Supreme Court Justice should trump (excuse the pun), our other hesitations. He has even organized a "faith advisory committee" comprised of some of the most respected Christian leaders in America. As a side note, I am appalled at the way the Body has treated the members of this committee and other evangelical heavy hitters who have endorsed Trump. We are willing to let Dr. Dobson dictate the way we raise our children, yet the instant he speaks out on a political issue, we mock him and call him a coward? We pay Kirk Cameron, our Hollywood hero, big bucks to go see his films, and then call him a sell out when he makes a comment about where we should place our vote? Maybe we should let our ruffled egos settle down for a moment and consider that we would willingly adhere to the wisdom of these men on any other issue. Even if you disagree with their political choice, please have the decency to treat them with the respect that their years of faithful service to the Kingdom have warranted.

This is the point in which many of you will be tempted to stop reading. I am going to take a moment to appeal to your common sense, and to address a few of the popular arguments that Christians throw out against Trump. No, these next few paragraphs are not from the Bible, but certainly practical wisdom is a Biblical precept.

PLEASE stop saying that failing to vote for Trump is not a vote for Hillarious...it is. I am truly not trying to insult your intelligence here. I simply fear you may be over-thinking things. No matter how much you attempt to pad your argument with mathematical or philosophical meanderings, the simple truth is that a third party NEVER has and CANNOT win the presidency, at least not in this election cycle's 2 party system, broken as it may be. (Yes, I am aware of Abraham Lincoln, but please don't forget that his election was not a three way split, it was a four way split.) Some of you have offered an unlikely equation that would enable a third party to steal enough votes to give the House the right to choose the president from among the top contenders. Maybe that would have worked if the Never Trump camp had been able to unify and rally around a singular third party candidate earlier on in the election cycle. This simply hasn't happened. Logically following, if only two viable contenders are in a competition, your failure to endorse one is implicit endorsement of the other.

Some of you have answered this argument by claiming that, "A vote for no one is a vote for no one," or, "by this logic, a failure to vote for Hillarious would be a vote for Trump," and thus, will choose to forgo the vote entirely. I would answer this contention by pointing out that a failure to proactively cast your vote against Hillarious means that she is one vote closer to winning the election. Your vote does matter. You are either helping to push her one step forward or one step backwards by your failure to act. You choose.

For those of you who argue that, "A vote for the lesser of two evils is still a vote for evil," I urge you to stop and think about the fallacious foundation of that statement as it applies to this circumstance. If abstaining from the vote entirely were a viable option in this election, then perhaps your well intentioned claim would hold its ground. As I have already demonstrated above, by not voting for one "evil" you ARE, like it or not, casting your vote for the other.

*Even if I accept your terms and define Hillarious as
the "big" evil and Trump as the "little" evil, you are
going to be endorsing an "evil" no matter WHAT you
do on Election Day. The difference is that one "evil"
has promised to do his best to protect your right to
worship freely, and one has promised to do everything
within her power to suppress them. You may argue
that Trump will turn tail and act against Christians
once elected. You are absolutely right. He could. We
can be CERTAIN, however, that Hillarious will do her
best to destroy what little sense of decency we have
left.*

*"But, but..." I can hear your continued protests and
growing disgust, "Trump is so, so...pompous, so
brash, so unfit for office." The disciples didn't
approve of the outsider who was doing their job either.
Jesus helped to correct their perspective. This wasn't
about them. This was about the future of the Kingdom.
I can still feel your eyes rolling at me but please listen.*

*I believe that a lot of the discontent over Trump is due
to his brash nature, yes, but also because of the blow
that was dealt to your pride when an outsider was able
to come in and usurp the leadership of your party. This
may not be true of you personally at all, but I am
certain that it is a large part of the driving force
behind the Never Trump movement. I am simply asking
that you examine your motives. If you detect pride as a
motivating factor, please pray to be released from it
and follow the example of Ben Carson. If anyone had a
bone to pick with Trump, it was Dr. Carson, but as he*

*so wisely stated in a Fox interview when asked how he
was able to get over the personal insults dealt him by
Trump, "If this was about me, I could never get over
it. This is about the future of our country."*

*This isn't about your personal likes or dislikes. This is
about the future of your children. If you aren't willing
to overcome your personal chagrin that an outsider
could come in and do your job for you, then you have
no one to blame but yourself when Mrs. Hillarious
Rodham Clinton is elected.*

*You will have lost the right to act as a martyr when
she comes after your right to speak freely about issues
such as homosexuality and the exclusivity of the
Gospel because you had your chance to do something
about it and you did NOTHING.*

*Some of you have chosen to avoid the conflict entirely,
and have decided to abstain from voting because no
matter the outcome, "God is in control." I agree 100%
that God is in control and that no matter who is
president, Jesus Christ is King. This overarching fact
that God reigns has NEVER been an excuse for
inaction. In 1 Timothy 2:2 we are commanded to pray,
"For kings and all those in authority, that we may live
peaceful and quiet lives in all godliness and holiness."
If we are to pray for a political environment that
fosters peaceful Gospel conversations, does it not
logically follow that if given the opportunity to help
make this a reality, we should act?*

This situation reminds me of the fable of the drowning

man who turned down three rescue attempts with the rationale that, "God would come and save him." When he drowned, he questioned God about why He would allow him to die. God responded with, "I sent you three boats!"

Whether we like it or not, America is drowning and the Trump boat, though less than desirable, is the only viable option for rescue that we have to keep us afloat for the time being.

In Cruz's address to the Republican convention, he repeatedly acknowledged the fact that this may be America's last chance to save herself. I beg you to consider the words of your own hero and make the only sensible choice.

If we do not vote for Trump and therefore vote for Hillarious, we will have lost our right to complain about the escalating murders of third trimester, unborn lives in America and the increasing span of The Parental Rights Organization, because we had our chance to do something and we did nothing.

If we do not vote for Trump and therefore vote for Hillarious, we will have lost our right to complain about future, liberal Supreme Court Rulings, because we had our chance to do something and we did nothing.

If we do not vote for Trump and therefore vote for Hillarious, we will have lost our right to complain when our pastors are imprisoned for hate speech crimes, because we had our chance to do something and we did nothing.

If we do not vote for Trump and therefore vote for Hillarious, we will have lost our right to complain when we lose our right to bear arms and fret over the safety of our families, because we had the chance to do something and we did nothing.

I am not arguing that Trump is a great man.

I am not even arguing that Trump is a good man.

I am arguing that in the words of Christ Himself, God can use an individual that is "not one of us" to further His purposes and protect His people.

I am arguing that in this time, and in this particular circumstance as the only nominee for Republican Party, Trump is the RIGHT man to serve as President of the United States.

Unless something cataclysmic occurs between then and now, he will be receiving my vote in November.

DISCLAIMER: As a friend of mine noted in her thought provoking blog, "This election season has been especially difficult for believers...Believers who are actively walking with Christ, and sincerely seeking His face on this issue, have come away with completely different conclusions on how they should vote in November." This being said, I understand that many fellow Christians will completely disagree with my interpretation of Scripture and will, in sincere conscience, choose to not vote for Trump. I want you to know that I still deeply respect and love you. My allegiance to the Kingdom of God completely outweighs my allegiance to any political party or leader. Let's not "eat each other alive in front of the world" guys. We are going to be Americans for only a short while. We are going to citizens of the Kingdom of God forever.

Unfortunately, I have been forced to publish this note anonymously to avoid the violent backlash that is certain to ensue. I am also certain some will call my intense tone throughout this article, "bullying." It is not my intent to bully. It is my intent to demonstrate what I believe to be the seriousness of this situation. Please do not equate my heartfelt cry with harassment. I, as well as you, have the right to be passionate in the expression of your beliefs. That's what America is supposed to be all about, isn't it? Despite our differing opinions, as stated above, I will continue to love, respect, and enjoy the friendship of my "Never Trumper" friends throughout and after the conclusion of this election cycle.

My conscience is clear before God because I have done all that I believe He has called me to in regards to this issue. Can you say the same?

29: THE SAGA OF THE DEPLORABALL

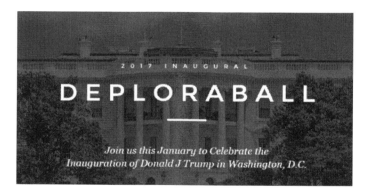

The Deploraball was always, at its heart, a group of friends holding a party to celebrate Trump's win. Though it vastly outgrew that original concept, from the start, all we wanted to do was get together with like-minded people, tell stories from the campaign trail, and raise a glass to a hard-fought victory together. Little did we know it would turn into one of the most controversial events of the entire year.

I live in the Washington DC area. Throughout the campaign, there were lots of opportunities for me to travel across the country to swing states, debate locations, and generally anywhere where we could find Trump or Hillary events to let people know what was going on in the race, and try to tell the true story from the ground level. I also got the chance to meet hundreds and thousands of amazing people through social media, and would occasionally later meet them in person at rallies or events around America. After Trump swamped Hillary on November 8th, people all started talking about coming to Washington DC for the inauguration. I thought, finally, everyone is coming to visit me and I don't have to sit in the car or on a flight for hours! As inauguration week plans began coming together, I started talking to a close group of friends of holding a meet-up for social media friends - mainly Mike Cernovich, Lucian Wintrich, and Jeff Giesea, among others. We picked a name "the Deploraball," and our idea was a "ball for us all" – a play on the fact that normally, the many inauguration balls are exclusive, invite-only affairs.

Initially, we were preparing to finalize a contract with Clarendon Ballroom for about 500 people, when the business suddenly reneged on our original proposal, refusing to host the private party. Dan Lamothe a reporter for the *Washington Post* tweeted out the e-vite for DeploraBall on Monday, noting, "Trump fans to hold 'Deploraball' at Clarendon Ballroom around inauguration. Various Breitbart/Infowars folks going." Following

Lamothe's tweet, the Clarendon Ballroom was inundated with hate comments from the left, attacking us a Nazis, homophobes, and every other name under the sun. The business then shifted into damage control mode, tweeting directly to media outlets in denial of any events "contracted" for January 19th.

Behind-the-scenes, I was contacted by reporters looking for a comment on the fact that we did not have a real event contracted, and they were asking if I had misrepresented the nature of the event with the Clarendon. I went back and looked at my emails, and every single one was signed with my title, Special Projects Director of Citizens for Trump. I had represented the event as an "inauguration celebration of the victory of Donald Trump." Clearly they were looking to discredit us, and were trying to make our audience think we were engaged in some kind of moneygrab without offering any actual event. That couldn't be further from the truth.

This attempt to discredit us as organizers of the event was immediately countered by us when we released the original paperwork from Clarendon, saying, "Here is proposal from Clarendon Ballroom for Deploraball. They are refusing to honor the proposal, won't host event."

Some still wonder why Trump won, and now you have the answer. We can't even have a party – open to everyone, including liberals, gays, blacks,

Latinos, whites, women, men, trans, and everyone else – without having Hillary supporters harass the venue owner to shut us down.

We had a hold on the date and were negotiating the proposal – we planned to sign a day before. Suddenly the venue called us up extremely angry and unwilling to work with us. It was all because *Washington Post* put pressure on them. Hillary voters never get no-platformed, but for some reason Trump supporters routinely do. There has been a concerted effort of harassment from businesses, governments, and social media companies discriminating against Trump supporters. This was like refusing to bake a cake for someone based on their personal beliefs.

Fortunately after the story got out, we had had so many more venues and event centers reach out to us who wanted our business and hundreds of guests, as well as some special guests who are now asking how they can be a part of the best inauguration party. We decided to double the size of the event to 1,000 people.

I took the opportunity to ruffle the feathers of low-info trolls and fake news media operatives alike by tweeting, "LOL no, guys, we are not going to have Deploraball at the Russian Embassy."

Deploraball then released the following official statement:

"After selling 500 tickets in just over 24 hours, the Deploraball learned that the venue hosting the event would not honor its proposal after they were harassed by Hillary supporters. The good news is that demand is far greater than expected, and the fecklessness of the venue means we can now have a larger party in a bigger venue. The Deploraball is still on. Details coming soon!"

Following that, we decided to fail-forward. We secured a new venue: the media's own hallowed National Press Club. The folks in the mainstream media had a conniption fit when we announced it. It was glorious. To their credit, the Press Club was totally accommodating of us, and great to work with throughout the process. They never treated us any differently because we were Trump supporters, unlike many other places. This would be later put to the test as the event date drew closer.

After we announced the National Press Club and released new tickets, it took less than 24 hours for the entire event to sell out. Everyone was talking about it as the hottest party at inauguration 2016. We knew we needed to put on a good event for everyone, and keep the budget as tight as we could to keep ticket costs down for all our guests. After all, this was supposed to be the people's party. We ended up securing a ton of great entertainment for the Deploraball – neo-folk singer Tatiana Moroz, viral superstar Scott Isbell, epic American flag live-painter Scott LoBaido, and Sheriff David Clarke agreed to stop by to greet the crowd. We even had a great photo booth with lots of costume props to take pictures with everyone.

It seemed like everything was going well. That was too good to be true.

Early on in preparation for the inauguration, we got word that a group of Hillary supporters was planning to cause chaos and riots in DC that week, and called themselves DisruptJ20 in reference to the inauguration date, January 20th. When I heard that they were holding some planning meetings in the DC area, I decided to head down myself to get a firsthand look at what they were up to, and things they had in store for all of our guests coming into town. After all, my own parents were planning to come down for the inauguration, and after all the violence against Trump supporters along the campaign trail, I was wary of what would come next at the inauguration.

In early January I went to my first DisruptJ20
meeting in the basement of an old church in DC.
The stench was unbearable. At first I thought a
sewer main had burst and was seeping into the room
somehow, but I soon realized it wasn't the sewer, it
was the lack of hygiene by most of the attendees at
the impromptu – literally underground – meetup.
About 150 people were there, and people of all
shapes and sizes. It was like a cross between a
Grateful Dead tailgate and a Weather Underground
rejects society. 70s-era anarchists mingled with
their modern SJW decedents, and they sat around in
circles discussing how to best prevent Donald
Trump from being inaugurated president, and how
to prevent anyone from celebrating it. It took me
about half hour to break down their organizational
hierarchy. It ran the gamut from Soros-recruited
paid organizers to rank and file college dropouts
and vagrants. I left at the end of the meeting, taking
with me a stack of documents and notes that
outlines their planned crimes for the week. There
were planning to: attack inauguration visitors at
subway station entrances, use rollerderby skaters to
harass guests, throw smoke bombs into crowds, and
even rig up quadcopter drones with bottle rockets
and conduct divebombings on the assembled
masses. Specifically, they also said they planned to
target the "Nazi Ball." I asked around what they
meant by that, and they explained they were going
to attack the Deploraball – our own event! I turned
over all this information the Press Club, who
handed it to the DC Police Department.

As I was getting ready for the next planning meeting, DisruptJ20 threw me a curveball. They released a public dossier of people they were targeting to attack at the Deploraball. The list included: MIKE CERNOVICH, JACK POSOBIEC, LAUREN SOUTHERN, CASSANDRA FAIRBANKS, BILL MITCHELL, STEPHEN LIMBAUGH, JOE BIGGS, ROGER STONE, JIM HOFT, LUCIAN WINTRICH, GAVIN MCINNES, and SCOTT ISBELL. I was honored to be among such company. The dossier quoted me saying that Star Wars Rogue One was an anti-Trump film. They were completely correct.

Still, they had burned me. I would be instantly recognized if I attended another meetup. Fortunately, James O'Keefe and the awesome people at Project Veritas stepped into the fray. They conducted an undercover investigation of DisruptJ20, and using their infamously-effective hidden camera interview technique, were about to get leaders of the plotters on tape divulging some of their plans for attacking the Deploraball.

"I was thinking of things that would ruin their evening, ruin their outfits and otherwise make it impossible to continue with their plans. So they get nothing accomplished," Scott Green, leader of the D.C. Anti-Fascist Coalition, said in the undercover video.

Another activist, identified as Luke Kuhn, said during a sit-down at the Comet Ping Pong pizza parlor in Northwest Washington, "If you had a pint of butyric acid, I don't care how big the building is, it is closing." Mr. Green responded: "And this stuff is very efficient, it's very, very smelly, and it lasts a long time. And you add the benefit, everybody is going to walk outside in the freezing cold," he said. These people were talking about using throwing butyric acid at my mother.

Thankfully, we had already planned a heightened internal security presence from the Press Club, and hired additional security personnel, but with the additional weight of the Veritas videos, the FBI and DC Police were alerted, and added layers of additional external security for the building and surrounding area. We really owe it to everyone's efforts there – without the police presence, the event would have been completely shut down. Just another example of the 'tolerant' left.

We released another statement: "With all the high-testosterone veterans and alphas attending, a protester would be foolish to try to infiltrate the party — but we are still taking every possibility seriousl."

"We are more likely to encounter protesters when getting into and out of the Press Club Building and at the check points for the security perimeter. If you encounter protesters, our strong recommendation is to not engage with them in any way. Take the high road. Do what you need to keep you and yours safe, but otherwise ignore them."

Make no mistake, what DisruptJ20 was discussing was liberal terrorism against our event – using violence to achieve a political means. After the videos were released, we found three of them on our guest list and revoked their tickets. The DC Police actually arrested the same three, who later pled guilty. Law and Order.

We were still wary of the way our event would be covered in the press, so we took great pains to make sure it was accurately covered by journalists. We granted press access to a number of publications, including the Washington Post, Politico, New Yorker, New York Magazine, FOX, Rebel Media, Breitbart, and RSBN. However, we declined access to CNN. Their reporting just wasn't up to our standards.

In response to CNN's press request we sent the following: "Dear CNN, We're hosting the Deploraball at the Press Club because we support quality journalism. Unfortunately, we feel your coverage during the election was biased to the point of being irresponsible. We question your integrity as an institution of journalism. Therefore we will not be issuing you press passes."

Sometimes tough love is what it takes for fake news to learn.

Then, came January 19th, the night of the Deploraball. I had pushed for the 19th as the date of the event because it was the eve of the inauguration, the night before Trump came into office. Most inaugural balls are traditionally held on the night of the inauguration itself, but I thought instead of competing for bandwidth, we could instead own the night of the 19th. It was also the end of the Obama era, and the beginning of the Trump era. What a magical evening it turned out to be.

Arriving early to the event, I didn't even have my tuxedo on yet. I first stopped by a few of DisruptJ20's known staging areas around DC to get an idea of their numbers, and I didn't want to stand out to them. OPSEC is everything. It didn't look like they had many people show up, and at that point I thought it was going to be a quiet night. Still, better safe than sorry. When I finally got to the Press Club, I entered through the main door after calling inside and verifying I really was Jack Posobiec. Photo ID required. No, this wasn't voting in Philadelphia, it was real security. They wanded me, checked my ID, and escorted me inside. Outside even hours before, police officers surrounded the building and stood ready to protect the attendees from the violent leftists threatening our First Amendment Right to Peaceably Assemble. I thanked as many of them as I possibly could.

Inside, I got changed in the bathroom, and left my bags and jacket downstairs and was required by security, then headed up to the 13th Floor for a pre-event dinner. I greeted many of the event organizers and was glad to see so many familiar faces there. Everyone looked tremendous in their evening best, people I had spent countless days with on the road, at flash mobs, in the middle of protests and riots, and everything in between. We went around the table and introduced ourselves. Everyone clapped when James O'Keefe entered. Just as dinner was being served and I had taken a few bites of steak, my phone started blowing up again.

Here we go, I thought. It was my parents downstairs, and they were having a problem getting inside – tying to pull up e-tickets from their smartphones. I called my mother, usually the most sensible one in a crisis, and in the background I could hear some kind of noise. I asked her what it was, and she exclaimed, "They're rioting! The smoke is going off!"

I bolted out of my seat and ran down the hallway to the elevator, frantically jabbing my finger at the button for the lobby floor. After what felt like an eternity, it finally deposited me on the ground level. I burst through the doors and bounded up the stairs

three-at-a-time to the main entrance, just as my
family was making their way through. I showed my
organizer pass to the internal security who waved
them inside. I made sure they were okay, and then
looked past them to the chaos beyond.

What had been a regular city street only an hour
before was transformed into a war zone.

A sea of disheveled, writhing rioters gathered
outside the National Press Club harassing out
partygoers, setting random fires everywhere and
vandalizing public sidewalks and streets. I hear the
rioters screaming "racists," "neo-Nazis" and
"fascists" attending our party. It's likely some of the
"protesters" were paid operatives, but the damage
inflicted they did was real. "Get Off Our Streets,
Nazi Scum!" My mother had just been out on this
street.

Some lit fires and threw eggs, while others threw
bottles and swung sticks at the back of partygoers'
heads. Others started fistfights while shouting,
"Screw our president!" Perhaps they were too
stoned to realize Obama was still president for
about another 15 hours.

The situation got so out of hand that Washington,
D.C. police fired pepper spray into the crowd to
disburse the anarchy. Police in full riot gear clashed
with hundreds of protesters Lacy MacAuley, lead
organizer of anarchist group DisruptJ20, lit

American flags on fire, chanting "And, we are dancing!"

I opened my iPhone and started Periscoping the event, trying to show the world what was going on in the present, and all I could even see in front of me was the sea of rioters. The street had completely disappeared. Suddenly, I heard a whizzing past my ear that reminded me of what it sounded like to be shot at. Training kicked in, and I bent my knees, dropping down. On the ground, I found the ammo. It wasn't a bullet, but a large D-Cell battery. It was quickly joined by others. "They're throwing D-Cells!" I narrated on the Periscope feed.

At that point security came up to me, ushering me inside. "Sir, you can't be here," they said, placing a hand on my shoulder.

"What do you mean I can't be here? This is my event," I called back.

"Sir, no, I mean you're in danger!"

He was right. I didn't want to stop periscoping, but the security situation was deteriorating. The longer I stayed out there, the more of a target we all became, and it was becoming even more dangerous for the security guards we had hired to protect us and our guests.

I stepped back into the foyer, just behind the glass doors. I could hear more large batteries clanging against the windows. Eggs exploded on the glass, their yellowed yolks slowly dripping down the bright façade of the National Press Club. It was becoming harder to see. Suddenly the door opened, and six foot five of tuxedo and quaffed silver hair appeared right in front of me. It was talk show host Bill Mitchell, arriving for the party.

"Bill!" I yelled. We had never met in real life before, but had talked over Twitter, and he'd had me on his show as a co-host many times over the campaign.

"Quick take my periscope!" I yelled, and threw my phone over the security guard standing between us. Kek was with us, because Bill caught the phone and held it up high above the fracas. "Its special guest cameraman Bill Mitchell!"

Bill panned the phone across the crowd of rioters as their ranks rippled and surged, smoke bombs cast a billowing gray plumes amidst the darkness, while fires burned in the street where the Antifa rioters set the American flag ablaze as their anger turned violent. Everyone needed to see what they had done to the streets of our capital city. After a few minutes, security pulled Bill in, too. The mob roared outside, deprived of their targets.

Inside, I talked to the security officials as people were being wanded, IDs checked, and directed up to the 13th Floor elevators. The problem was, there were still hundreds of ticketholders outside in the cold January air waiting to get past the riots. The DC Police came up with an idea that reminded me of the ancient Roman phalanx. The police held the partygoers down the street and around the corner from the violence, out of harm's way. Then, they formed a human barrier of police in riot shields, body armor, and helmets around groups of ten or so decked out in eveningwear dresses and tuxedoes, and slowly escorted them to the entrance, one group at a time. This slow, but necessary, process made us push back our planned speaking program from 8pm until 10pm.

Despite the torturous scenes outside, inside the atmosphere was euphoric. The Deploraball was a family affair, because we were a family. It was the first time in my life I've ever been around hundreds of people I'd never met before, but everyone felt like family. To me, the whole event felt like it ended as soon as it began, the hours simply flew by and it was over as soon as I realized it had started. The Press Club put together a great spread of food for the event, and there were multiple open bars around the event spaces.

We had reserved the entire Press Club, so there were many different rooms, each one a sort of unique experience. One was like a large bar atmosphere, another like a cocktail reception. Some were smaller comfortable sitting areas with light music – I took the chance to stop by the piano at one point to tinkle the ivories. The main room at Deploraball started out as a dance floor complete with a DJ and amazing live performance by Tatiana Moroz and Scott Isbell. Then, the main hall turned into an impromptu Trump rally, with numerous people taking to the stage to speak on coming inauguration of Donald Trump, and the movement that brought us all together.

In my own speech, I made reference to the fact that how remarkable it was, that even with everything going out outside on the street, everyone inside was happy, warm, and celebrating. It was fitting, I said, because we've had to fight every step of the way to get to this day. Every day on the campaign was a street fight against the Left, the media, the establishment, even physical violence, and we had still overcome it. Its not hard to win the argument when you have truth on your side. I also recounted the fact that I personally had been interviewed the morning of the Deploraball by the US Secret Service regarding allegations made against me by radical left-wing blog Buzzfeed. The result of which, was us all determining that that Buzzfeed was fake news. I closed my speech by referring to a

John Adams letter he had written in 1818,
explaining the American Revolution to a friend:

"The American Revolution was not a common
event. Its effects and consequences have already
been awful over a great part of the globe. And when
and where are they to cease? But what do we mean
by the American Revolution? Do we mean the
American war? The Revolution was effected before
the war commenced. The Revolution was in the
minds and hearts of the people; a change in their
religious sentiments of their duties and obligations."

What they called the American Revolution in 1776
might be referred to as the Nationalism Revolution
in 2016. 240 years after the original revolution,
Americans once again decided they were fed up
with how their government was treating them, that
they wanted more for their lives and their families,
and decided to take political steps with fight back
against forces of globalism and corporate
conformity that Hillary Clinton represented. She
called us "Deplorables," in defiance. We embraced
it, and wore it as a badge of honor. We held the
Deploraball to celebrate the victory of the
Deplorables, the little people, the regular, ordinary
Americans who gave their energy, their time, their
efforts, and their voice to the cause. In the end, we
took our country back.

EPILOGUE: AND IN THE END

To many people the appeal of Donald Trump will forever remain a mystery. They simply will not, for a variety of reasons, allow themselves to consider anything he or his supporters say as a reasonable statement. Many refer to this as "Trump Derangement syndrome" - The inability of Trump haters to listen to, discuss, or even have a discourse with someone who is a Trump supporter. This book is not about those people. Those people can be found on the left and the right, they can be found in academia, big journalism, corporate America, the office, the bar, the campus, and just about all over California. If you know someone like that, and I'm sure you do, I propose the following suggestion:

once you're done reading this Book, give a copy of it to them. And say the following, I know you don't like Trump, but you have to admit there must be some reason all those people voted for him. Now I'm sure all of those people are going to say something like "sure, all the racists voted for him, and all the idiots voted for him," and then cross their arms and lean back with a smug look on their faces. Then you respond, "Ok, but if that's true, we have you surrounded. And we have the presidency."

Donald Trump came to win the presidency with a movement of simple national pride and commonsense solutions to complex problems. There is no other explanation really needed for his win. The groundswell of support for Donald Trump was not nearly for Donald Trump the person. This is why numerous attempts to knock Trump out of the race only further galvanized Trump supporters. Instead, Trump supporters saw themselves as fighting to take back their country from special interest and multinational corporation's but had long since taking over the reins of power in America. The movement was and remains a movement i've regular ordinary people who gave their own time money and resources in efforts to elect Donald Trump not for his at his sake, but because they saw The price of another corporatist president as being too high for themselves and for their children.

While the media and the Left were fixated on viewing Trump and Trump supporters through a lens of hatred and anger, it was really their own hatred and anger they were projecting. They view the world with extreme pessimism and negativity, so it is no surprise they view President Trump with the same darkness.

After traveling to over a dozen Trump rallies across the country, and so many flash mobs, the RNC, the debates, and the inauguration, I can say without a doubt that Trump supporters are not motivated by hate. Spend any time with them and I guarantee they will be some of the most positive, uplifting environments you will ever find in your life, even if you aren't a MAGA-hat-wearing Trump supporter. Trump supporters are motivated by love. Love of their nation, love of their fellow man, love of those who put themselves in harm's way, and love of trolling normies top kek all star sup /pol/ life comes at you fast big if true #deplorable #MAGA3X #TedCruzDidHarambe #HillarysStools #SpiritCooking #DumpStarWars #TrumpCup #DeusVult #SlavRight #PraiseKek #FreeKekistan #REEEEEEEEEEE

50099648R00132

Made in the USA
San Bernardino, CA
13 June 2017